**Campus Whisper
Networks**

Campus Whisper Networks

Knowing with Sexual Assault Survivors

JANET HINSON SHOPE AND RICHARD PRINGLE

Rutgers University Press

New Brunswick, Camden, and Newark, New Jersey

London

Rutgers University Press is a department of Rutgers, The State University of New Jersey, one of the leading public research universities in the nation. By publishing worldwide, it furthers the University's mission of dedication to excellence in teaching, scholarship, research, and clinical care.

ISBN 978-1-9788-4503-9 (cloth)
ISBN 978-1-9788-4502-2 (paper)
ISBN 978-1-9788-4504-6 (epub)

Cataloging-in-publication data is available from the Library of Congress.
LCCN 2025030594

A British Cataloging-in-Publication record for this book is available from the British Library.
Copyright © 2026 by Janet Hinson Shope and Richard Pringle

References to internet websites (URLs) were accurate at the time of writing. Neither the author nor Rutgers University Press is responsible for URLs that may have expired or changed since the manuscript was prepared.

♾ The paper used in this publication meets the requirements of the American National Standard for Information Sciences—Permanence of Paper for Printed Library Materials, ANSI Z39.48-1992.

rutgersuniversitypress.org

For who dare tell, or someday may, and for who dare listen.

Contents

**Campus Whisper
Networks**

Introduction

How to Hear a Story

There are a million ways I've told. On my bed, in an essay, holding hands in an empty parking lot, in the middle of a sexual encounter, in a text. Not a single one has gone how I wanted it to. All have been awkward. I have yet to hear a response that I liked or even felt the slightest bit better from. I am not sure I will ever get one. I have accepted that it's just a shitty thing that comes from rape—something I would have never expected to be so hard. But somewhere along the way, it turned from a sobbing list of broad scope terms in no particular order, to a clear, concise narrative used to explain my life track, to a calm collected story about how it has made me the person I am today. Each little, imperfect, red-faced telling has helped take out the trauma bit by bit until it has simply become a respectful acknowledgement of the person I was at that time. I am grateful for every single person that has been a listening ear, for they have allowed me to heal. (Kali)[1]

Over the years, dozens of students, almost all of whom are women or nonbinary/genderqueer, have shared their stories of sexual assault with us: before college, during college, while studying aboard, on and off campus. Our bearing witness is hardly unique.[2] Most women, and some men, know someone who has been assaulted: a teammate, friend, sister, coworker, cousin, lover, and/or spouse—or perhaps mother, father, brother, or child. Most often, this knowledge remains a well-guarded secret, a confidence shared during a private moment of vulnerability and pain that, with time, may emerge, as Kali shares, into an understanding more complete and stories more widely shared. We have seen that most women and gender-nonconforming students (and fewer men) here at our college do tell someone about their experience. However, the timing varies, and the telling may not initially resemble a story.[3]

The tellings and stories students have shared with us, pointing again to the prevalence of sexual assault in their community, are but a small fraction of their tellings: they have told one another, Title IX staff, counselors, peer listeners, and faculty and staff. They have shared experiences and support in survivors' groups and at annual Speak Outs; they have organized artistic exhibits, panel discussions, and consultations. They have written in literary magazines and conducted research projects summarizing peer interviews. They probably have spoken and written to friends and family and other survivors off campus and back home or at similar academic institutions. Some have even posted about their experiences on social media. After her first college party, Kali told her close friends in a private social media posting. Initially, she made light of what happened to her, but her friends, "devastated" by the post, told her immediately that what had occurred was not okay. Over the next few days, she told others in her inner circle: a roommate and her boyfriend. With time, she would find the courage to tell her parents as part of the context for her decision to transfer to another college. Far from being confined to an incident between two people, her rape set in motion a relational tsunami that moved through her networks and community. However, from the university's perspective, there was nothing to know, no record that the rape had occurred, no knowledge of its impact within the community. Like most students, Kali chose not to report her rape to college officials; Kali says the very thought that there would be a record of her rape "shook me to my core."

Sexual assault within student communities has been and continues to be pervasive, impactful, and largely unacknowledged, tucked out of sight—a pattern that has been replicated over time and across American colleges and universities. Decades of convergent research about sexual assault pervasiveness have yet to generate collective uptake and understanding, let alone deep community engagement, on college campuses. As Mary Koss noted some years ago, "One questions what it is going to take to convince people that rape on campuses is serious when the siren has been on for 25 years."[4] College administrators and presidents continue to downplay the prevalence of sexual assault on campuses, seemingly unaware of how it affects more than those students assaulted and how it reverberates through an entire community.

How does so much knowledge about sexual assault experienced by students remain below the surface of formal discourse? This book focuses on how members of a college community acquire relational knowledge of sexual assaults experienced by its students and the implications of knowing and not knowing, both for students and for the college community. We examine how knowledge about students' sexual assaults within the community circulates and how cultural and institutional systems channel disclosures and narrative accounts away from the commons along rule-driven, communicative pathways that favor secrecy, silence, and not-knowing. As a result of this channeling, knowledge (or epistemic) gaps exist laterally within the student community, fracturing student awareness, and vertically between students and college officials, distorting institutional awareness. This dynamic, both a product of and a contributor to epistemic injustice, limits our ability to imagine and design practices that mitigate the harms inflicted on survivors and on the college community.[5]

In the following chapters, we explore the nature and implications of these durable knowledge gaps, focusing on the lateral gaps among students in chapters 2 through 5 and the vertical gaps between students and college officials in chapter 6. First, we must clarify what we mean by relational knowing via telling and listening and what we mean by an epistemic field of sexual assault, one that is structured and managed.

Relational Knowing: The Power of Telling

> She sits in my office, eyes cast downward; I get a sinking feeling that I know what she will tell me about why she is struggling to attend class and turn her work in on time. Her soft and halting words gather momentum as she shifts in her seat. I have been on the receiving end of this story too many times. She tells me a family member sexually assaulted her, and she is having nightmares. I listen and offer alternative ways for her to complete her assignments.
>
> Fast forward a few months, and a first-year student acknowledges that she might be off to a rough start. When I ask a few probing questions, she tells me she was raped the summer before she started college. I notice the scars on her arms, some old, some freshly cut. We talk about the impact of the experience; she never talks about it with me again. Later in her academic career, those scars will be covered by brightly colored tattoos that tell a different story. (Told by Janet)

Letting someone know about an assault can take many forms, including verbal and nonverbal *tells* in a person's affect, posture, or habits from which an astute observer and close friend might surmise something has happened.[6] Depending on how familiar the observer is with the person—a roommate, say—they may even be able to piece together a loose narrative involving when, where, what, and so on. In this way, an astute, concerned observer might gain insight into the person's state of mind, giving rise to empathy and understanding, which might lead to questions, conversation, and/or intervention. However, even in this sort of minimalist conveyance of information, a trusting relationship is required for the shared information to become knowledge if something has happened or something is amiss. A tell, such as Kali's social media post, a student's missing assignments, averted gaze and halting voice, might become a telling. This conversation relates or imparts principal components of a storied incident to one or more listeners if the listener is attentive and receptive. Janet's reminiscences are examples of astute listening/observing that invited the students to say more.[7] Had they not said more, Janet would still have been compassionately suspicious, given the tells. Alternatively, then again, tells might be missed entirely, or misinterpreted or ignored—there are many reasons why even best friends and faculty might instead "look the other way."

Though there are many ways to know about sexual assault, including through socialization, direct experience, testimonies of others, and educational instruction, we have come to understand that all ways of knowing do not carry the same power. Our relational knowledge of, or our awakening to, within-student-community sexual assault came via the connections we forged with student survivors and their committed allies. Even so, we kept looking for more objective evidence of sexual assault pervasiveness to establish an unassailable fact and to bridge what we assumed were the critical knowledge gaps within the college community, as if certified statistics themselves would awaken the college to its moral imperative. However, of course, *knowledge of* an issue does not have the same transformational capacity as *knowledge with*—knowledge gleaned from an interpersonal encounter, one that leaves a sticky, embodied residue produced by mutual affect, reciprocity, and interrelational agency, what we refer to as relational knowledge. We prefer to think of this kind of knowing as more than knowing-that and more than knowing-how.[8] Even though one can acquire propositional knowledge of sexual assault (such as knowing that it occurs), and procedural knowledge (such as knowing how to resist it or report it), these forms of knowing, while important, do not have the same impact on individuals, as relational knowing. It takes much more concerted and persistent effort for sexual assault knowledge to become deep and intimate, a kind of knowledge that can transform and inspire people and communities.[9] Knowledge-of permits moral/ethical and emotional distancing; one in four as a statistic need not be *felt*—locally, immediately, interpersonally, or communally. Hearing it, one need not empathize or be called viscerally and cognitively into a radical rethinking of one's immediate community, complicity, personhood, or responsibility to the speaker. Knowledge-of is less likely to upend social imaginaries built around sexual violence and less likely to upend one's sense of residing in a "safe community." This distancing may help explain why, in the face of the one in four statistic being widely known and cited, fewer than one-third of college presidents thought sexual assault was prevalent at American colleges and universities and only a minority reported it was prevalent at their institutions (Jaschik and Lederman 2015).

Knowing-with, or relational knowing, is the form of knowledge production that has the most power to rattle one's sense of reality—the power to disrupt. As such, it should not be surprising to find it closely regulated. It is discursive, suggestive, metaphorical, and supported by systems of relatedness and shared meaning making that hold affective qualities and sensibilities.[10] It is the heart and soul of stories—the power in the testimonies shared during Speak Outs such as Take Back the Night. Knowing-with is embodied and felt, and while it cannot be subsumed under rationality, it operates as a powerful analytic tool with transformative potential for students and their community. Tellings are the primary way that persons acquire relational knowledge. They invite the listener to know-with and are not simply one-way information transmissions.[11]

In keeping with the fraught complexity of conveying an experience of sexual assault, we prefer *telling* over "disclosure" or "notification" to highlight the relational dynamics and the structures of power that influence the exchange and shape the very possibility of an exchange. Tellings foreground the aspects and complexities of talk and narration that pertain to relating, sharing, and confiding to confidants in a social/political context. Tellings of assault, however incomplete they might be, are storied and relational, and as such they convey experiences *of* and *within* the social world (Alcoff 2018).

In much of the research on sexual assault disclosures, the telling is conceived to be propositional—a secret divulged. Further, the information exchange is assumed dyadic, moving one way from survivor to recipient, and the recipient's role is reactive, having positive or negative valence for the survivor's clarity, well-being, and agency, and conceived as having affective consequences for the recipient. In this way, a disclosure is akin to a signal crossing a synapse, and the research focus is on the conditions favoring or disfavoring the crossing and the short- and long-term consequences to the survivor and/or to the recipient. In other words, the secret content is "transmitted." If transmitted to an official, that person is "notified" and the conveyance is considered a formal disclosure.

More than a one-way transmission of information, a telling involves at least one other person (often more), hence its relationality. The active listener, whom we call the confidant, is more than a passive recipient of information, more than a terminus in a notification sequence, even when one prefers to think of it that way.[12] What transpires in a telling is more than a delivery of propositions— that is, first this, then this. How the listener engages with the telling has significant implications for the community's relational dynamic and the construction and circulation of knowledge. Tellings are leaps of faith fraught with risks, including exposure, misunderstanding, and unintended, sometimes far-reaching, social/relational consequences, such as community rupture.

The Epistemic Field of Sexual Assaults Experienced by Students

If tellings direct our attention to the relational knowledge held by the survivors and confidants who compose the whisper networks that exist within campus communities, the existence of specific telling patterns points to a knowledge structure that directs within-community sexual assault tellings, sometimes filtering them, sometimes channeling and routing them to dead-ends or blocking them at the source. This knowledge structure, which constitutes the local epistemic field of sexual assault, regulates the flow of relational knowledge within community discourse, and it is governed by seen and unseen impediments and proclivities that serve particular interests. This structure is marked by policies and procedures, roles and statuses, and norms codified and uncodified in formal and informal social interaction sites within the campus community. These structural levies are strong and rarely breached. Fast-rising torrents of tellings, such as when student activists demanded Title IX changes, are rare. If they occur, they can reshape the field to a degree.[13]

The uneven contours of the epistemic field fracture a student and college community's self-awareness, giving rise to discrete knowledge loops within relatively isolated communicative networks (Bailey 2014). Some in the college community can observe and experience more than others, and some of those are more able than others to share what they know within relational networks. Some in the community hold greater power, authority, and credibility than others, and their power and privilege bestow epistemological blinders that predispose them to the vice of not needing to know (Medina 2013) and, in some cases, wanting to not know. There are many strictures that formally and informally govern whom one can tell, how and when one can tell them, and, once told, what one can and cannot do with the information.

Discrete epistemological communities are segregated within and along fissures in the epistemological field. For example, the tellings of survivors and their confidants do not rise to the surface often and hence remain out of earshot of college officials and students who are not members of their peer networks. Given the many social/political, legal, and policy impediments to speaking about the problem, asking about it, and otherwise sharing stories and information, keeping one's story below the surface and mainly inaudible to those outside the whisper network confers some safety, albeit with considerable personal and community costs.

The epistemological field also includes those who are unaware, the "avoiders," those students (and staff) who know of no student within their community who has experienced an assault or sexual violence since enrolling at the college—they have, so far, managed to avoid encountering this feature of the community. Many reasons account for their unknowing, both the passive ignorance that results from limited opportunities and impediments to gaining knowledge and the active ignorance that is a product of the unwillingness to seek this information (Medina 2013). Systemic misogyny, rape myths, and individual and institutional self-interests feed both forms of ignorance. In sharing what we know about sexual assault, we often encounter silence or disinterest, even wariness among community members, all which function to secure epistemological blinders. Sometimes this disinterest or wariness is expressed as shock or disbelief, such as "this cannot be true because I would have known" or "I had no idea this was occurring." Sometimes, people justify their ignorance and disinterest: "it is not my business to know"; "only certain people should know, and I cannot share what I know." Members of privileged racial groups often react similarly to the loud and ever-present alarms signaling racial injustice and brutality. We are often reminded that knowing relationally those things we would rather not know and are not supposed to know is not easy. We all have blind spots; those things we would rather not know or do not need to know because they do not affect us. The responsibility to know our ethical epistemic obligations is what makes a just community. Institutions of higher education should be at the forefront of this endeavor.

To better understand the epistemic field, we use relational knowing scales as legends of sorts to map and measure the field's lateral unevenness among students. For example, some of our survey scales differentiate between those students who have no knowledge of peers within the community who have been sexually assaulted and those who know of others or who have received a telling personally. The scale shows that slightly more than one-third of students who inhabit the field possess no relational knowledge of sexual assault within their community. At the same time, the remaining nearly two-thirds know of someone who has been assaulted and/or are survivors themselves. This triadic partitioning of relational knowledge is a robust and consistent finding, and we refer to our scales' ability to map the epistemic field in this way as the "rule of thirds." As we will discuss, the rule of thirds affects how students perceive and experience their college.

Left unaware of the possibility and proximity of sexual assault, of its presence and impact among one's peers, it would be difficult to perceive sexual assault within the community as a collective rather than an individual tragedy. Moreover, sans hearing of it from others, unless one were to experience it firsthand, it would be difficult to perceive it at all. In this way, the existent, local, epistemic field of sexual assault, as it runs laterally among students, blocks personal knowledge from becoming social knowledge (Medina 2013).

Our Research: The Connection Between Individual and Representational Stories

We share the context around our research and privilege stories and tellings to point to the capacity of tellings to birth a significant representational story. These tellings are not only about a singular institution or even about a singular, unjust, epistemic field. They are not the academic purview of a single discipline drawing insights from philosophy, gender studies, psychology, and sociology. Crosscutting disciplines and institutional types, these tellings have expansive meanings and implications for other colleges and universities, and indeed other kinds of communities. Our own research-origin story, as we will discuss, can be traced back to a small group of committed students who approached Rick with a set of questions about the prevalence of sexual assault within their college community. They proposed a survey that included not only the key "Have you experienced . . . ?" questions but also "Do you know other students at (institution) who have experienced . . . ?" questions. It allowed them (and us across subsequent surveys) to parse student participants into varying levels of awareness about the presence of sexual assault within their community. We further developed their line of inquiry across subsequent surveys by focusing on the patterns and pathways of tellings and by asking about the meaning and experiences of telling and hearing about sexual assault within the student community. As researchers committed to multimethod approaches, we provided opportunities for students to elaborate, in their own words, on their responses to these questions.[14] The following chapters feature their clarity and eloquence, as well as pieces of their stories.

While we privilege stories and tellings in students' own words, we cannot deny that the quantitative data we have collected are also clear and eloquent and featured prominently, albeit occasionally, across the chapters. Not surprisingly, the stories the quantitative data tell dovetail strikingly with those told directly by students. While statistics and graphs and the quantitative values that undergird them may not seem relational per se, they can, with attentiveness and discernment, and within a mixed-methods approach, illuminate the power and importance of knowing-with.

Our story is local, yet the problem and the patterns discerned are not merely local. They likely resonate with other communities. We would not be surprised to learn of other students at other institutions approaching faculty for advice and support to document "properly" an insidious, unacknowledged harm. Subjugated knowledge is always a site of resistance imbued with possibilities for change. To help keep this local story tethered explicitly to the larger representational one, we integrate findings from climate surveys of American universities (Association of American Universities 2017, 2020) and national Clery data to demonstrate that the sexual assault awareness gaps we describe as part of the local epistemological field are likely present at other colleges and universities.[15] Though these fields have contours specific to the communities in which they emerge, the norms and rules associated with speaking about sexual assault to confidants and to authorities cut across institutions.

Outline of the Book

Chapter 1 examines relational knowledge in greater depth by foregrounding tellings as key to understanding the circulation of knowledge and how various norms, both formal and informal, restrict tellings. A telling is more than an exchange of information that produces a reaction and much more than a cognitive phenomenon. A telling represents a passage through a relational portal that brings others "into the know," thus growing the circle of knowers and making it harder for those in the circle to ignore and/or minimize the effects of sexual assault on individual students and their college communities.

We describe the patterns and trajectories of tellings: who tells whom and when. Contrary to depicting survivors as silent, most survivors tell someone about the incident relatively soon. We trace the tellings patterns to understand better how knowledge circulates within specific networks. Identifying these telling pathways makes visible how knowledge flows through a community and leads to specific knowledge loops—that is, who is "in the know" and how formal and informal norms shape who is told and how. Social rules or norms, what we call telling rules, dictate what can be said, when it can be said, to whom, and how it should be conveyed. These rules also apply to how one listens, what Medina (2013) and Fricker (cited in Dieleman 2012) discuss as virtuous hearing and the obligations of the hearer to the survivor and their story.

Chapter 2 begins to map the epistemic field around sexual assault on college campuses. The field is composed of two planes, formal and informal. It is structured and managed, and regardless of intentionality, it limits community awareness. Some forms of knowledge, propositional and procedural, flow more freely. The relatively free-flowing circulation of this type of knowledge attests to its relatively benign nature; it does not upend the prevailing discourse of sexual assault nor expose the paradox. Individuals within a community can know a lot about an issue while knowing very little about its effects within a community, specifically its fractures and woundedness.

This chapter describes how vertical gaps between the informal and formal discursive spaces and lateral gaps within the undercommons—the informal, unofficial discursive spaces—produce an uneven knowledge field. Groups within the structure are situated differently for their ways of knowing. Some hold a great deal of knowledge gleaned from personal experience and/or relationally through experiences shared with them. The relational knowledge that emerges from these tellings impacts them personally and shapes how they experience and perceive the institution; thus, it carries transformative potential. Others within the system possess no relational knowledge of the proximity of sexual assaults. Consequently, they lack an awareness of the fractures and woundedness that exist within the community due to this kind of violence.

These knowledge groups seemingly live in different local realities. We draw upon Association of American Universities (AAU) data (2017, 2020) to demonstrate that these kinds of epistemic fractures exist at other colleges and universities. In this chapter, we introduce the use of the rule of thirds to measure and depict the different realities experienced by students. In this way, we highlight and prelude the power of knowing with survivors, knowing relationally, to reshape the knowledge field in the service of justice.

Chapter 3 uses quantitative data and patterns to examine how membership in an epistemological community influences how a student perceives sexual assault within the college and how the impact of sexual violence spreads within the community. Since seeing can often convey more than words, we include visual representations of the relational scales to represent the significance of relational knowing. This chapter begins to unpack the groups who are situated differently along the relational knowing scale, beginning with the avoiders, those students who know no one within the college community who has been assaulted. Also, unlike the avoiders, those who possess relational knowledge of sexual assault or sexual violence within the community are negatively affected. It is not just the survivors who suffer; those peers who have received a telling, the confidants, are impacted by the telling, and their views of the institution are also changed, sometimes even more than survivors. Like the survivors, the silver lining is that they become more informed, empathic, and agentic regarding the issue. They are potential change agents, a finding we will return to in the conclusion.

Chapter 4 examines the whisper networks between survivor and peer/friend in the undercommons to understand better the testimonial muting that occurs. We explore why survivors share their experiences with a friend and how telling affects the survivor and the friend. Telling is a shared meaning-making endeavor, and survivors and friends describe how meaning is jointly constructed. Trust emerges as an essential property of relational knowing, and informal telling rules associated with privacy and confidentiality guard this secret. Tellings within the whisper network represent a knowledge loop that differs from the knowledge pathways present in formal discursive spaces.

Chapter 5 turns its attention toward another epistemological group, the silence holders. Silence holders have experienced an assault since enrolling, but apart from their admission on our survey, they have not told anyone about the assault. A few of them are genuinely isolated with their experience in that they know no one else in the community who has been assaulted, but most of them do know of others. Paradoxically, most silence holders are "in the know" about others' experiences but have not shared their own. Many of them explained their reasons for not telling, which provides a map of the many social complexities student survivors face. Some are unable to define their experience at the time of the survey in ways that align with cultural and institutional definitions of assault. Some students find assault so quotidian that it is dismissed as ordinary, the price one pays for being a woman or gender-nonconforming. The chapter discusses how they plan to handle their experience: individually, expediently, and privately.

Chapter 6 focuses on the official knowledge of the institution. Much of what is known about sexual assault on college campuses and universities is based on the "official knowledge" gleaned through formal discursive practices. Knowledge in this realm of the epistemological field emphasizes the procedural information in policies and processes that direct individuals to specific knowledge channels. Title IX regulations define what constitutes official or actual knowledge of sexual assault. We integrate findings from the AAU climate survey surveys and national Clery data to demonstrate that the vertical gaps we describe as part of our local epistemological field are most likely present at other colleges and universities. Title IX's emphasis on procedural knowledge, with its focus on neutrality and select bits of information wrested free from the assault story, is at odds with what is required for students to trust and for colleges to be viewed as trustworthy. This emphasis is often at odds with relational knowing. The college's official knowledge of sexual assault within the student community is governed and routed by notification policies and procedures that render, categorize, and adjudicate student tellings into confidential and individualized endpoints. Within the official reporting channels, the friendship rules that guide tellings among students, anchored in close relational ties, are set aside in favor of notification templates. Students who enter the formal process often feel betrayed by this profound rule reversal, the institution's management and restriction of relational knowledge, and its willful ignorance of the community's wounds.

Though Title IX processes are intended to funnel more tellings to formal spaces, students are reluctant to engage. As evidenced by the vertical gaps, these channels convey very little knowledge circulating in the undercommons.

In the conclusion, we discuss how and why relational knowing matters and how and why lack of awareness and active unknowing can sometimes give way to awareness, understanding, and agency. How might colleges and universities support the development of relational knowing through their efforts to increase awareness? How might the epistemic field be refashioned to increase the flow of relational knowledge, thereby growing the network of knowers? Title IX, taking a downstream approach, is unable to generate enough community uptake about sexual assault and sexual violence to produce change and create widespread student trust. Moreover, within the carceral orientation of Title IX, culpability, responsibility, and care are individual traits, not community properties. Within that frame, there are no lessons for the larger community and no opportunities to see, understand, and heal community fractures and wounds.

1

The Secret World
of "Tellings"

Decades of research document the prevalence of sexual assault among college students and its underreporting to college officials. Tellings to authorities such as a Title IX administrator, a public safety officer, a faculty member, or other mandated reporter are the formal tellings that officials and administrators recognize and emphasize as the sine qua non for legitimacy, veracity, and institutional responsiveness. Other tellings to the friend, partner, mentor, teacher, or family member, referred to as "informal disclosures" in the research literature, occupy a secondary status to formal tellings. These tellings are barely audible, merely whispered utterances in private spaces, the backstage of social life—rumor and gossip, perhaps. It is not surprising, given the emphasis on formal tellings, that survivors are often described in the media as silent—though most survivors on college campuses have told others, just not those who count. In the recent 2017 Association of American Universities survey of college students at thirty-three universities, 86 percent of women, 79 percent of men, and 83 percent of LGBTQI students who were assaulted had told at least one other person. Similarly, in our surveys, most students assaulted, 72 percent, have told someone, most often a friend. Far from being inaudible, these whispers constitute the background din, the roar that reverberates within the undercommons—the informal space occupied by students in the know. In writing about the reluctance to talk about sexual violence, Francisco (2000) contends that if the occurrence of sexual violence were audibly present in our daily lives, "its decibel level equal to its frequency, it would overpower our days and nights,

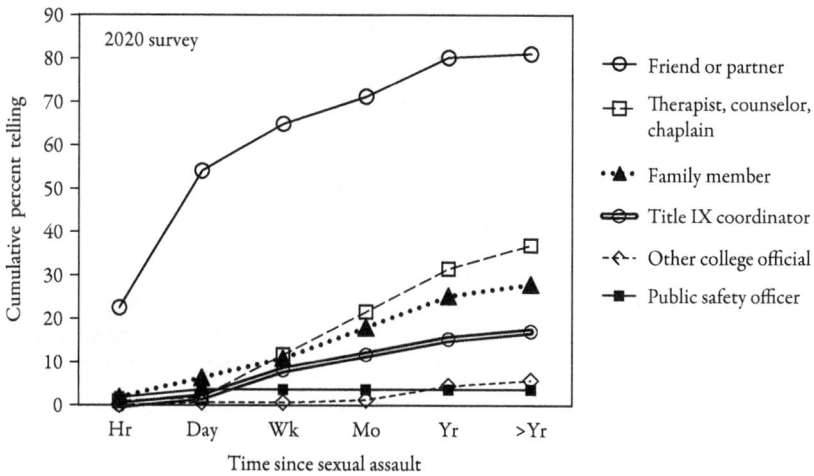

FIGURE 1 Whom and when survivors tell. Cumulative percentage of whom and when survivors tell.

interrupt our meals, our bedtime stories, howl behind our lovemaking, an insistent jackhammer of distress" (2). It is this roar, this jackhammer, the campus community seems determined not to hear.

Telling Patterns

Who do you tell when something disrupts or shatters your sense of self, others, and your social world? What resources do you tap? And when? Our surveys indicate that student survivors' tellings follow a distinct chronological pattern. Figure 1 shows, for our 2020 survey, the cumulative proportions of survivors who had told someone within various elapsed-time intervals since being assaulted, ranging from within an hour after the incident to more than a year later.[1] The top line in the chart pertains to telling a friend. Survivors told friends often and soon. For example, over half had told a friend within the first day, and over 80 percent had told a friend at some point by the time of our survey. Parents, therapists, and Title IX officers, shown as separate lines, were told less often and later, if at all.

Survivors turn to friends or peers as their trusted confidants relatively soon after the incident. Sarah shares, "I told my friend over breakfast the next morning, which was when we divulged the night's events." When we asked in the climate survey, almost 70 percent of survivors had told a friend. Based upon our surveys, 20 percent of those experiencing sexual assault (defined behaviorally) tell a friend within one hour of the incident. Practically no one else gets told within that short time. The likelihood of telling a friend increases steeply throughout the day and the week and slows over time but continues to increase throughout the year and beyond. For some survivors, friends are the only witnesses to their experience, at least "for now." Kerri adds, "I only told my closest friend here, [and] even though she had a positive response, I didn't want to tell anyone else."

Contrast telling friends with telling others. As shown in Figure 1, practically speaking only family members, other than a friend, are sometimes told within the first day. The likelihood of telling a family member increases steadily but slowly over time. Between a month and a year, it is overtaken by the likelihood of telling a therapist, counselor, or chaplain. The likelihood of telling a public safety officer or other college official stays very low, though the latter two register a slight increase over time. The likelihood of telling a Title IX coordinator is higher; it also shows a slow but steady increase, to the point that 12 percent of those who have experienced an assault have told a Title IX coordinator by the time we surveyed.

By the time of the survey, many survivors had told others besides their friends. An analysis of the order of tellings (not shown in Figure 1) revealed another pattern consistent across surveys: if someone tells only one person, it is almost always a friend, and if someone tells more than one person, they almost always tell a friend first. Family members, if told at all, tend to come second, and therapists or counselors, if told, tend to come second or third. A small percentage of students opt to tell Title IX officials. When they do, it typically occurs later and after, or synchronous with, other telling resources— 2.8 resources on average, suggesting Title IX consultation and reporting happen on the far end of other conversations. Tapping other resources on and off campus, such as public safety officers, is far less common, as shown in Figure 1, leveling off at less than 10 percent by the time of our survey.

Similar telling patterns appear to exist at other colleges and universities. Friends or peers are overwhelmingly the recipients of tellings, and only a small percentage of students elect to tell a college official, a finding we will discuss in chapter 6. Embedded in student descriptions of tellings are implicit norms that govern the appropriate recipient of this kind of personal, difficult information, how it is managed, and if it is shared with others. We have become mindful of the many norms that set boundaries and rules on whom we talk to and what kinds of talk are permitted to this person, in one context or another. We have come to understand the impact of these norms on how relational knowledge about sexual assault circulates within the local epistemic field.

Invisible Fences: Telling Rules and Frames

While Rick was walking, he noticed a small, blue metallic sign at the corner of a well-manicured lawn: "Dog contained by invisible fence." "Aren't we all," he thought. Knowing, telling, and being told are social phenomena, and norms associated with social interactions and organizations shape information transmission (or nontransmission) (Ryan 2006). As social participants, our interactional responsibilities include knowing what others want and need to know, and how others expect this knowledge to be conveyed. Understanding these rules also includes knowing the tensions and contradictions within these various forces and how to navigate among them. As a social theorist, Erving Goffman (1983) was particularly attuned to the invisible fences that govern interpersonal interactions, including communicative exchanges. He understood the importance of these ground rules, called traffic codes, that come into play in anticipation of or when spoken interaction occurs. Like the well-manicured lawn, these unseen fences are a feature of social tidiness; they provide some order to social interactions.

Telling rules also apply to how knowledge moves through organizations; some, but not all, are codified in policy and law. These norms, what Ryan (2006) calls notification norms, determine who needs to be told what, when they should be told, and how they ought to be told.[2] What happens, however, when the aim is not the need to know, as Ryan discusses, but the need to not-know, the need to regulate the transmission of specific information or knowledge? We use *telling rules* to encompass the regulation of telling and not telling, for both speaker and hearer, for individuals and the community. Telling rules channel information along discursive routes that create loops and uneven repositories of knowing and not knowing. As a result of these rules, understandings prevail as "to when and where it will be permissible to initiate talk among whom, and by means of what topics of communication" (Goffman 1983, 34). Speaker and listener enact telling rules. Depending on the context and the relationship of speaker to listener, the rules are enforced informally or formally.

Many telling rules are so ingrained, so deeply intertwined with our socialization into socially competent adults, that people enact them without much thought. Like avoiding an invisible electric fence, their actions seem natural, resulting from individual volition. So accustomed to the perimeter of their social yards, individuals do not think much about how they regulate their speech patterns and behaviors. However, if one spends time with young children, one is reminded of the unfettered nature of talk before one learns what is taboo—little children should not say "swear" words—and with whom one can share specific information. Recall the lessons children are taught early on about not sharing personal information with strangers. They learn quickly what is private and that private means only certain people can know. Furthermore, they learn to guard family secrets. Most social participants understand the cautions against indiscriminately "airing one's dirty laundry" and the negative reactions if one shares too much information (TMI in modern parlance; Vangelisti et al. 2001). Certain topics are best suited for select audiences, and individuals who pry into discreet matters are reminded "it is none of your business" (Bellman 1981).

For matters of great seriousness, people might need additional socialization or training about conveying certain information. Doctors are taught how to deliver bad news (Fallowfield 1993; Francis and Robertson 2023); friends learn how to communicate empathy through their words and comportment (Goldfarb 2020). Faculty might be trained on how to respond to a sexual assault telling. As social beings, we learn that certain topics are best discussed in designated settings with behaviors and speech registers congruous with the emotional valence of the topic. We also learn to avoid culturally charged topics, except among the closest of social relationships. Recently, for example, Megan Markle (2020), the Duchess of Sussex, wrote a *New York Times* op-ed about her miscarriage, calling attention to the prohibitions that regulate the sharing of personal information. Some conversations, she writes, remain taboo despite the "staggering commonality of the pain."

These rules apply to tellings about self but also govern how we receive information about others and what we *do* with the information. Early messages about what it means to keep a secret, to be a tattletale, or to gossip enforce the telling rules for sharing information about others. In social groups, individuals learn that sharing private information about others, often called gossip, has deleterious effects on close relationships. Adherence to these rules, particularly among those with close ties, carries a relational obligation, a moral duty of sorts (Cowan 2020). In the *Metaphysics of Morals*, Kant (2017) references these rules in his discussion of friendship—specifically, the moral duty to protect our friends' secrets.[3] When it comes to sex talk, a multiplicity of telling rules come into play.

Sex Talk: The Dynamic Multiplicity of Rules

The focus of a telling, the "what," has implications for whether an individual tells someone and, if they do, whom, how, and when. Likewise, it has implications for how such tellings are received. Previous research has shown that specific topics are often avoided—indicating the presence of telling rules. Young adults, for instance, avoid discussions with their parents around relationship issues, negative life experiences, friendships, dating, and sexual experiences (Guerrero and Afifi 1995; Afifi and Afifi 2009). Persons are more likely to practice avoidance with opposite-gender recipients around issues of sexuality or sexual experience (Guerrero and Afifi 1995). Other studies show that individuals are hesitant to share stressful information with others to manage the impact on them, a form of protective buffering (Joseph and Afifi 2010). In describing the difficulty of telling others about her rape, Francisco (2000) acknowledges that part of her hesitancy included her sense of responsibility for introducing pain into the conversation: "I'm often aware of causing discomfort, of the conversation collapsing into silence, and wishing in those moments, I had kept quiet" (20).

In American culture, talk about sex, like race talk, seems especially charged; it is considered private and confidential, a topic engaged with select others in particular contexts or not talked about at all. Euphemisms for sex-related words, such as the "f-word," the birds and the bees, sexual misconduct, private parts, and so forth, signal this verbal avoidance (Zerubavel 2006). Speaking to one's child about sex is sometimes referred to as "the talk," acknowledging its necessity on the one hand and its difficult, off-path nature on the other.[4] The requirement by some colleges that sexual consent be ongoing and verbally given, an example of an institutionally adopted telling rule, points to a perceived need for direct sex talk while also acknowledging that such talk is "off path." "Perceiving the need for" is itself a disruption in the epistemic field, indicating that some within the community have noticed a dangerous knowledge lacuna and are seeking a way to fill it. Women at Antioch College in 1990 perceived the need and pressed for policy change. They imagined consent talk, while unpracticed and awkward, would be more than transactional, more than propositional. It would instead be, in our terms, relational and knowing *with* one another in the moment. On this side of the #MeToo movement, it is easy to see this as a beautiful vision, not something to be mocked. Still, for young adults in the hookup culture, talking honestly and relationally while risking "catching feelings" (Wade 2017) are not necessarily welcome aspects of the hookup. In hookup culture, communication that includes knowing-with is seen as potentially destructive to the success of the encounter (Freitas 2013)—hence the reason the term "hookup" is so ambiguous and has so many meanings. Ambiguity is the point. Maximizing ambiguity opens possibilities but can also shroud and legitimize predation.

The *Saturday Night Live* skit in 1993 and the myriad other venues mocking Antioch College's consent policy over the years illustrate the deep-seated cultural resistance to the very idea that people might talk openly about their sexual intentions and that ambiguity can be problematic and dangerous.[5] Even today, the notions that caring deeply for one another should be, could be, intrinsic to intimate encounters and that talking honestly about desires and consent should be the rule can seem absurd. There are reasons for sex to be subjugated at the level of language (Foucault 2019), particularly if repression operates as an assurance that there is "nothing to see, nothing to know, and nothing to say" about such things. In this way, repression masks oppression.

While the epistemic field in which tellings circulate is malleable—that is, change happens, as per evolving notions of consent—the field is still largely shaped by power and privilege and hence is resistant to change, especially transformative change. When Antioch challenged ways of knowing, the deep resistance manifested as nationwide scoffing and mockery, which ensured no immediate emulation by other colleges. As Foucault (1980) warned, knowledge/power and language go hand in hand. As part of this evolving power edifice, or truth regime, telling rules about privacy, privilege, race, gender and sexuality, autonomy, and individualism regulate the discursive spaces around sex, in general, and sexual assault, in particular. Official reporting policies are there to channel and filter the talk, and their attendant officers and experts oversee the process and curate the reports. If one must talk about sexual assault, there are more and less appropriate ways to engage the conversation and more and less appropriate people to tell. As perceived needs for truthful speech emerge and shift within the community's whisper networks, stressing the governing rules, the shifts are shaped as a kind of rear-guard action to follow the contours of the deep-seated rules. As Foucault (2019) explains, power is best understood as the multiplicity of force relations. These force relations are, in our usage, the multiplicity of rules, many contradictory, some formally codified in policies or law, others enacted relationally, but many chained, linked, and regulated systemically to favor the status quo. Telling rules are often designed to protect others, both the individual and the institution, and in limited ways they undoubtedly do. Individuals within the community weigh moment to moment, to know or not, to tell/listen or not, in a manner that consistently yields the rule of thirds and, for the most part, a quiet commons. Their overall effect, however, is to uphold the arrangements that keep within-community sexual assault hidden from community view.

Telling Rule Frames

Telling rules, enforced formally or informally, depend on the context, one's role in the community, and the relationship of the speaker to hearer. Faculty and staff are familiar with formal campus telling rules codified as nondisclosure agreements, the professional confidentiality codes of conduct for clergy and therapists, and the mandatory reporting required of responsible employees. As Alcoff (2018, 151) describes, norms dictate who speaks, who assumes the role of the audience, what kinds of statements may be shared, and how these tellings are interpreted and used. Some norms are explicit, but others, particularly those in informal settings, are regulated by implicit conventions around the social identity and status of participants: their age, race, gender, sexuality, and relationship. Student comments about tellings by the speaker/survivor and the hearer/confidant point to the normative properties that regulate tellings, who is most appropriate to receive this telling, how one manages the information, and if it is shared with others. Most recipients of tellings, the friends, understand that the telling is shared in confidence and not meant to be told to others. Sometimes, the survivor explicitly asks the confidant to keep this confidential. Gwen explains, "In this incident, and in every other incident which has been disclosed to me, these people asked me not to share. They wanted to just transfer out and not let it follow them. They didn't want people to know that this had happened to them." Others understand that this type of knowledge about another is not meant to be circulated, that it's not their story to tell, or, as Valeria put it, that "it's not my place to speak on an issue that isn't mine." As we will discuss in greater depth in chapter 4, friends understand their obligations to the teller: chiefly, this is the kind of information one keeps confidential.

For other audiences, the telling rules may shift. Telling a family member, if it occurs, happens later. There are rules tied to specific audiences. Kareema clearly explains the rules that apply to telling her parents about her rape.

> I knew the rule I had to tell my mom in person, because if she knew and couldn't hold me immediately after, her mamma bear instincts would cause her to explode. So, I asked her to come down for the day. I lived kinda close to the school, something I used to resent, but at that moment I was glad to live close to campus. The rules of the disclosure were hard because there cannot be a right way to tell your mom you were raped. I hugged her hello and desperately searched for a place where we could be alone so I could get the words out. The place ended up being in her car. She must have known something was wrong. Moms always know. I told her, and she was upset, but she kept it together for me. That was another rule: the listener has to keep it together for the teller, because the teller is the vulnerable one. (Kareema's personal reflection, 2019, shared with permission)

Kareema told her mother before telling her father, a finding supported by previous research that shows that when children talk about a sexual topic with a parent they are more likely to discuss with the same gender parent. Kareema acknowledges it was "trickier" to tell her dad. She describes telling her dad outside her parents' home:

> My dad was really the tricky one, less so my mom. At least she understood the injustice that came with being a woman, the feeling of being scared of a man. But my dad? I didn't even want my dad to know I was a sexual being. So, standing there outside my house with my mom, watching him get mad, I was worried the anger was directed toward my sexuality. As if he was angry I grew up, as if staying his little girl would protect me better. I reasonably knew he was mad at the situation, but it was my situation. It was my body making him upset. I found myself in the moment wishing I could be better for my dad. If I were better, or smarter, or stealthier, I would not have been raped. If I were stronger or more resilient, I would be able to stay on campus. . . . Although we never addressed it again, I know my parents still feel the pain. I know they both physically and emotionally, literally and figuratively relive that talk every day.

Kareema's account of her telling her dad reveals how hard it is for survivors to avoid the blame and shame that follow a sexual violation. Moreover, it reveals how the hearer's reaction, in this case her dad's anger, surfaces a range of emotional reactions. Even though Kareema acknowledges the emotional pain that she and her parents share, neither party mentions it again.

Speaking about sexual violation typically falls in the category of excluded speech, and as Alcoff (2018) notes, the exclusion is often based on grounds that it is too disturbing or that no one wants to hear about it.[6] Stories of sexual assault are too stigmatizing, too traumatizing, too triggering, too sexual, too ambiguous, too litigious, to name a few rules disguised as cautions, to be talked about freely and publicly.

Talking about one's assault, whether to a friend or parent, to a Title IX officer, or to a congressional committee, or passing along what we know secondhand to our colleagues, impromptu, is disruptive, with the potential to unsettle everything: agendas, relationships, college plans, communities, and existing gender and power dynamics. Often, the disruptive potential is contained, if not altogether thwarted, because of the myriad ways tellings are muffled and deflected and tellers escorted back into line. Assaults themselves are too often framed as private, aberrant incidents, and one's experience is just that, one's own, or worse, imagined, and tellings within the commons are deemed indiscrete, impolite, and aberrant.

Breaking the Rules

I'm sitting in a small meeting room with colleagues I trust, discussing the program and agenda. We move off track, sharing classroom stories, referring to beloved students we know well. One colleague asks, bemused, "What happened to Shea? She was a star in my classes. Her work is 'all over the place'!"

"She was raped!" I blurted.

Silence. . . .

I see their pained shock, their eyes downcast. I am embarrassed and ashamed.

Silence. . . .

Slowly, we return to the agenda; Shea is not discussed again. (Told by Rick)

What happened here? Prior to this gathering, Rick was witness to a semipublic telling by Shea and consequently held relational knowledge of the incident and her personal upheaval. Was her telling public? Not really, though it happened abruptly and unexpectedly in a classroom. Everyone in the class might reasonably have assumed they had been entrusted with the story—that it was told to them in confidence—but that was not made explicit. In the later incident with his colleagues, Rick "disclosed" a truncated version of Shea's experience into an ungarnished declarative. Even though his conveyance was propositional and traveled one way to unprepared recipients, we consider it a *telling* due to the relational and power dynamics present in and outside the meeting and the classroom. Also, Rick's comments connected dots and stitched the outline of a story and explanation regarding the seemingly downward turn in Shea's classroom performance. The affective and relational reverberations of the telling were palpable within the meeting and likely continued long afterward—certainly so for Rick:

> My shame and regret are partly that I likely betrayed Shea's confidence and trust, partly that my colleagues would likely agree, and partly that I blindsided them with hurtful information. At the time I was irritated that my colleagues seemed to have missed a "tell" and were seemingly poised to attribute Shea's lapse to an irresponsible wobble in her normal, commendable, steady-state comportment. I was defending her. Also, I was already frustrated that the faculty and staff communities had seemingly not taken to heart our telling them, a year earlier, based upon our survey findings, that they should be ready to be compassionately suspicious of sexual assault whenever they notice alarming changes in a student's behavior. Still, I'm embarrassed I didn't say more gently and indirectly what needed to be said and say it in a manner less harmful and in a way that might have encouraged discussion—maybe agency—instead of discomfort and silence. And I'm disappointed I was irritated with colleagues I respect when I know from my own experience how easy it is to project blame-narratives onto student lapses. It's difficult to keep in mind that students walk daily through minefields, as do we all. (Rick)

Rick's regrets, wrapped in shame, embarrassment, and disappointment, are subjective indicators of rule violations. The silencing within the room, the downcast eyes were relational indicators he had ventured off path, and the ensuing silence and negative, long-lasting emotions testify to how difficult it is to navigate this epistemological landscape. The discomforts and disconnections arising within that moment and lingering still were epistemic fences at work, delimiting shared awareness, discussion, understanding, and action. Shea's story, however truncated, presented a moral dilemma. It was her story, and yet it was also a representational story. An opportunity to confront the issue was lost, a familiar ending to a familiar tale.

Though shame was the registry of Rick's rule violation, relatively benign in his case as a sitting tenured professor at the time and in the company of friends, Alcoff (2018) lists some of the externally imposed, often severe, chastisements that tellers can expect: "Survivors are sanctioned, fined, suspended, or expelled from school and heavily criticized if they venture out to unofficial, unmanaged avenues, such as social media, anonymous graffiti, or art activism. As more survivors are speaking, the terrain of struggle has become the speech itself and the attempt to confine it within venues and modes that authorities find palatable" (49).

Currently, new students learn at orientation that their college has procedures for talking about sexual assault that include following a formal process. The process is laden with rules, including some that are tacit. For example, students are to understand that if they use the process, and if things "do not go their way," they are supposed to accept it and be quiet about it and not carry a mattress around on their back, as Emma Sulkowicz did their senior year, whenever on campus at Columbia University, until they graduated in 2015.[7] Nor are they to tell others about their assault and the institution's handling of it, or to post about it on social media like the Skidmore College student who was suspended from the college for a semester for this form of in-the-commons telling (Donegan 2021). Moreover, when repeat harassers continue to be employed in media/publication positions, even after multiple tellings fail to generate uptake and remedy, women are not allowed to create and post a Google spreadsheet, "Shitty Men," to circulate as a warning to women, as Moira Donegan did, for which she lost her job and lost friends.[8] These truth tellers violated tacit telling rules and suffered criticism, notoriety, and, in some cases, severe consequences. Invisible fences make themselves known when folks misstep. As faculty or staff venture into telling-rule violations to support a student, friend, or colleague, they might be reminded of nondisclosure agreements or of their institutional role at the college as a mandatory reporter—a very specific telling rule that compels, routes, and sculpts disclosures into dead-end tallies.

Dotson (2015) explains that when encountering an unfamiliar, disruptive telling, the first response is to reject it. The second reaction is to villainize it, and the third is to deny its possibility by making it a problem with the speaker or the study rather than something that is known and widely shared. We would add another response to Dotson's list: encase the telling in a protective layer of secrecy and redirect the knowledge along dead-end pathways away from the commons.

Conclusion

As more and more survivors and their allies have spoken about sexual assault, on this side of #MeToo and related truth tellings,[9] regulation policies have expanded proportionately. Survivor speech is increasingly channeled and constrained, made permissible within certain registers—as a secret, a therapeutic confessional, a legal or administrative charge or complaint. Of course, survivors are always welcome to "handle it on their own." Tellings, within this power/knowledge governing scheme, should they occur at all, require expert interpreters or mediators to render them acceptable and useful (Alcoff 2018; Foucault 1980).

If spoken at all, tellings are best whispered, in confidence, to trusted friends who understand they are to guard the secret, or they are told in confidence to officials, who render and channel them to various endpoints, away from the commons. Indeed, efforts to channel knowledge about sexual assault, part structural, cultural, and interpersonal, prevent information about sexual assault from entering community self-awareness. The community is thereby prevented from knowing-with. If information stays fragmented, limited to acquaintances alone and/or shunted into one or more official endpoints, the link between telling and the community's knowing is lost (Fricker 2007). Sexual assault on college campuses is sustained not by a conspiracy of silence but by a conspiracy of secrecy protected and governed by the local epistemic field. In the next chapter, we discuss the epistemic field. We begin with the dilemma faced by three seniors: how to awaken the community to the insidiousness of sexual assault within the student community without violating telling rules.

2

The Uneven Relational-Knowledge Field

In this chapter, we consider what it means to know and not know about sexual assault within the community. What is a knowledge gap, and what does it mean to close it? We begin by juxtaposing our earliest questions that focused on sexual assault prevalence with our later, emergent questions about how relational knowledge moves laterally and vertically through a community's local epistemic field and how it is often restricted from doing so. Thereafter, we segue to mapping the relational knowledge field, attending especially to the lateral uneven awareness that persists among students, the rule of thirds, and the attendant student-community fractures.

Our research journey began in 2008 when Rick met with Jenna, a psychology student interested in conducting a survey to measure the prevalence of sexual assault at the college. Speaking for herself and two other seniors (Paige and Leah), Jenna was frustrated by the mismatches between what many students knew to be true—that sexual assault was prevalent at the school—and what many of their peers and the college officially knew to be true—that reports of sexual assault were rare.[1] The issue seemed one of credibility. Whose knowledge was a better gauge of the extent of sexual assault on campus? Rick was sympathetic to the students' desire to settle the matter with a well-constructed student survey and agreed to help. He pointed the students to Koss and colleagues' (1987) survey design and findings, asked them to include qualitative questions, and helped them receive academic credit for their work. They designed a climate survey that tapped incidents, prevalence, and student awareness. They found, unsurprisingly, that the prevalence of sexual assault was higher than the college's official counts and seemed comparable to survey results at other schools. They also found that many peers were aware of other students at the college who had been assaulted since enrolling.[2] These two knowledge gaps, the vertical gap between students and the college officially and the lateral gap among students themselves, both pointed to high prevalence: many students had been assaulted since enrolling. One might think that would have settled the issue, that the students and the college community heard their siren call and mobilized. But nothing much changed.

We share this tale as the origin story for the years of follow-up climate surveys about sexual violence that we and others have codesigned and conducted to give credit to the original researchers,[3] and because their original questions and findings prelude our own and led us, eventually, to move past the prevalence question to ask instead, "Why and how do these gaps persist?" From that vantage point, we could see that the vertical and lateral gaps are landmarks within a contested epistemic field.

We also share the origin story to explore its deeper meanings, and we will return to it occasionally in subsequent chapters. For now, in its simplest form, the story tells of three students sounding a community alarm responsibly, being careful to adhere to local telling rules. Their questions emerged from their frustration with how the college's knowledge seemed to trump theirs. They were aware of how students' relational knowledge could always be overruled by the official counts, tallied in secrecy, the so-called hard evidence, and that the official way students were to notify the college of sexual assaults was to file individualized reports in confidence.

Because the college is small and residential, and because, as seniors, the students had lived on campus for years, they knew that sexual assault was prevalent and that its prevalence was a problem for students and the community. Their positionality afforded them a particular vista into the reality of campus life occluded from others occupying different positions within the college. Their sensibilities about the prevalence of assault arose as a by-product of their relational knowledge or knowing with their peers. In contrast, the college's official knowledge relied on reports, despite evidence indicating most students choose not to notify officials. The epistemic and moral frictions that come with relating to others led the students to question how one acquires knowledge about sexual assault within a community or fails to do so.

Given the college's knowledge regime, how could these seniors responsibly alert the community to this problem? They knew well enough that, as young adults, students, and women, they would have to speak the official language— the rational language of propositions, objectivity, and hard evidence—to have any chance of being deemed credible by college officials and skeptical peers.

They knew they would need an "expert" to certify they did it right. They chose Rick.

Given the mission of colleges and universities to expose students to new ideas, new ways of thinking, and trustworthy methodologies, it's not surprising that these committed students would assume the lateral gaps among students and the vertical gaps between student knowledge in the undercommons and official, institutional knowledge were fundamentally informational and that once reliable information became available, the gaps and inconsistencies would disappear. We initially shared their hopes, and perhaps we still do, to a degree, as evidenced by this research endeavor. We have sometimes slipped into thinking that closing the gaps is straightforward: more or better information, and that if you report the facts, people will hear you, and the community will acknowledge and tackle the problem. We thought "better data" might settle the matter, that survey data might garner the credibility in the academy's knowledge hierarchy that our experiences and students' individualized experiences lacked, and that the knowledge gaps might be filled or bridged. Of course, this story is not that simple. Despite many surveys and prevalence reports, the epistemic field remains much like what the students documented in 2009.

The Uneven Knowledge Field

What do we mean by the epistemic field of sexual assault? This field refers to the tellings and listenings about student sexual assaults experienced since enrolling. Our surveys, since 2015, asked about sexual assaults and sexual violence experienced directly or indirectly by current students since enrolling, and if and how they share that information. When asked "Did you tell someone?" and "Did anyone tell you?," the tellings and the relational knowledge that the tellings convey pertain to the local student community. Consequently, the relational knowledge that moves laterally by students talking and listening to one another pertains to within-community incidents and experiences.

Relational knowledge, as used here, is quite different from the evolving cultural backdrop that shapes general awareness and knowledge of sexual assault, the sexual assault imaginary, that students bring with them to campus. High-profile rape and harassment cases, legislation, and documentaries about campus sexual assault, as well as pre-K–12 curricula, have increased general awareness of sexual assault's pervasiveness. Students, faculty, and staff know that sexual assault happens in the world, including on college campuses. However, an awareness that sexual assault occurs in the world, or even in college or in one's past, is different from relationally knowing of its prevalence and impact within one's immediate community. Certainly, within-community knowledge gaps exist elsewhere, too, but to the extent they do, they are bounded by the features of those local communities, such as schools or neighborhoods, where people know one another and see each other as belonging. Defining the gaps as *local* and *within-community* distinguishes them from more prevalent but more abstract and potentially more "distant" awareness of sexual violence based upon such indicators as state and federal legislation, crime reports, regular media attention, and social movements (e.g., #MeToo). Is one's own local community safe? Some members may experience it as safe, even while others know it is not in particular ways. Some may know that sexual assaults have occurred to community members, and some may not. And, of course, some within the community have experienced sexual assault personally.

It is the uneven circulation of relational knowledge of within-community sexual assault, sometimes diverted, channeled, and collected to stagnate in small pools, that creates epistemic gaps of consequence within the community. As explained, sometimes the gaps are lateral—such as gaps in students' awareness of sexual assault within their community: their dorm, team, or friends. Other times, the unevenness is vertical or hierarchical—such as the gap between many students' experiences and administrative leadership's awareness and understanding. The local sexual assault awareness field can be uneven up and down an institutional hierarchy.[4]

A second important distinction needs reiteration here: knowing relationally of sexual assault within one's immediate community is different from knowing of it abstractly, as in the number of adjudicated cases or statistical summaries. When students tell one another and listen to one another, they share aspects of their lived experiences, inviting one another into intimacy and care, with particulars. The exchange is not a one-way notification but rather a conversation. The more abstract knowledge of local sexual assault, as expressed using a summary statistic, such as "one in four," or a Clery tally, such as there were two incidents of assault reported the preceding year, does not invite or compel relational attunement and empathy. Such summaries lack context and relatedness and render the survivors invisible and voiceless.

Minding the Gaps: Mapping the Relational Knowledge Field

Jenna, Paige, and Leah were relationally aware of the prevalence of sexual assault among their peers and aware of persistent knowledge gaps that existed within the campus community. It's as if they and some of their peers noticed a deep chasm in the middle of the quad. "How can you not see what we see?" they asked. "How is it possible for you to be oblivious to our own community's open wound?" Much like the tale of the emperor with no clothes, they were willing to name the obvious to point out the chasm. They also knew that gaps existed among students. Their survey confirmed statistically and restated propositionally what they had already surmised relationally. Building on their insights and with the aid of additional questions in subsequent surveys, we were able to map the knowledge field within which the vertical and lateral gaps reside as landmarks.

London subway riders are cautioned to mind the gap as they exit the train and to pay attention to the smallest of gaps so as not to be harmed. Social philosophers also use the metaphor of the gap or lacuna to refer to epistemic disruptions and discontinuities. Often, the metaphor of the gap or lacuna implies an emptiness or space. However, a total absence of knowledge about sexual violence, even local violence, is hard to imagine given the public discourse following the #MeToo, #YouAreNotAlone, #KnowYourTitleIX social media campaigns. Rather than simply conceiving the gap as a singular void, or even more simplistically, as a break in an information flow, we prefer lacuna's secondary meaning: pits or cavities in an anatomical structure, typically the bone. This meaning directs our attention to the structured bumpiness of knowing and suggests an unlevel or in this case an *uneven* knowledge field (Bailey 2014) rather than a linear vacancy, break, or distortion. Attending to the local sexual assault knowledge field and its lacunae might offer opportunities to see how the gaps are structured and related—to examine how knowledge about sexual assault is curtailed, deflected, and controlled using the many rules discussed earlier.

An uneven knowledge field within a campus community suggests a pattern whereby some people in a community know more than others and may know differently than others, and that the community itself structures the circulation of knowledge and awareness around sexual assault within the community. The structure that manages the circulation of knowledge points to social/ relational power dynamics and hidden fences. Some information flows freely, some is restricted, if not totally blocked, and some is carefully routed via channels within the field. Telling rules are part of this governance. The unevenness of the field also implies that some people are more positioned or entitled to knowing than others.

We have argued that relational tellings and relational knowledge do not move vertically from students to college administrators, almost by definition. In the first place, college officials are not often told. When told, the stories must be analyzed in relation to policy infractions or educational disadvantages where select narrative elements are evaluated against preset categories, prohibitions, and permissible adjustments. This is a carceral, adjudicating, evaluative framework of telling/listening that bears little resemblance to tellings among friends. While telling health and counseling officials might be expected to be more relational and contextualized, and hence more complete and more relationally responsive, they, like tellings to other officials, are held in strict confidence and individualized. We think of vertical tellings as being routed to dead ends— decontextualized, individualized, anonymized, and ultimately rendered into tallies or cases closed. Because relational knowledge does not often move vertically, the vertical relational knowledge gap is profound. The student researchers faced this conundrum: how to tell the community what they knew relationally. Our rule of thirds is a map of relational knowledge gaps, a relational knowledge scale. We will return to vertical gaps in chapter 6 after we explore the meaning and consequences of knowing relationally among students.

Relational Knowledge Among Students: The Rule of Thirds

Our first attempts at capturing relational knowledge relied on Jenna and her student collaborators' insights that it was important to tap students' awareness of other students who had been sexually assaulted within their community. Their data highlighted the lateral gaps in student awareness and led directly to our rule of thirds: across all subsequent surveys, slightly fewer than two-thirds of our students, since enrolling, either have been assaulted or know other students at the college who have.[5] Another feature of student awareness is that nearly all students (87.3 percent) who have personally experienced sexual assault know others in the community who have. Students often tell one another, and they often listen and believe. But not all students are privy to hearing and believing. The rule of thirds emerges from the unevenness of this lateral information flow.

Because the rule of thirds implicates students talking and listening to one another, we began to think of it as not only registering students' perceived proximity to sexual assault (i.e.., their personal risk within the community) but also registering their connectedness to community members' shared experience. The rule of thirds is based on relational-knowing scales that tap one's involvement in the whispered discourse about sexual assault within one's peer community.

We began to track tellings more carefully by adding new survey questions: "Did you tell someone? And, if so, whom and when?" Though obvious in hindsight, tellings do not often follow the official, regulated paths. Rather, they move laterally among students by word of mouth or "whisper networks." As noted, almost everyone tells, and they mostly tell friends they trust. They implicitly entrust their confidants to gauge who does and does not need to know their secret. The stories seep laterally, relationally, on a need-to-know basis.

Although some climate surveys ask survivors a few questions about whom they told, no surveys of which we are aware at the time have directed questions to the recipients of the tellings, the secret keepers and confidants. Curious about the relational dynamic and context, we added questions that probed the tellings themselves and what it means to be the recipient of a telling from a friend, in confidence—to be the listener, the confidant. In these ways, we continued to shift our focus from establishing prevalence and context to examining how community members become aware or not and, if not, what stands in their way.

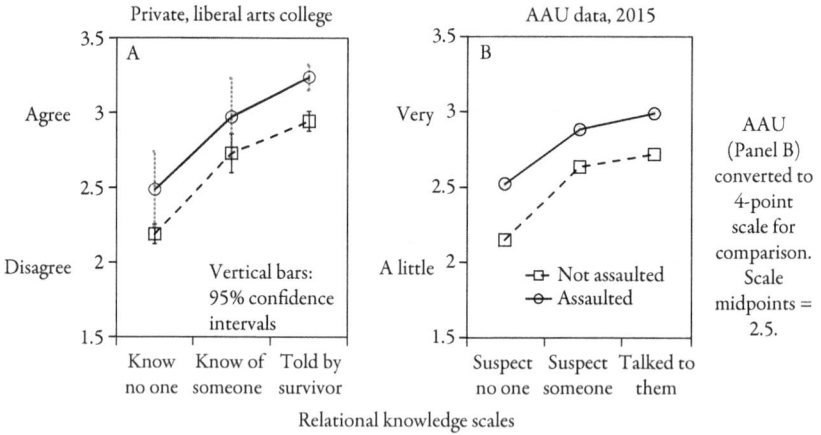

FIGURE 2 Sexual assault is a problem on campus. Agree/disagree sexual assault is a problem on campus (Panel A), or sexual assault/misconduct is problematic at the university (Panel B), by relational knowledge of other students' experiences.

This shift foregrounds the roughly two-thirds of the community who have not experienced sexual assault. What do they know about sexual assault and violence within the community, and how do they come to know?

Since 2015, we have asked survey participants to gauge their agreement or disagreement with assertions about the community. One item is, "Sexual assault is a problem on this campus." Not surprisingly, students who have been sexually assaulted since enrolling agree with the statement more than the students who have not. What did surprise us was that *knowing someone* in the community who had been assaulted was sometimes a more powerful determinant of one's agreement with the statement than was whether one had been assaulted, and receiving a personal telling from someone in the community was a still greater determinant. Students come to know about within-community sexual assault—and understand it is a problem on campus—by hearing directly from other students. The rule of thirds results from students talking to students they trust and the college remaining silent on the issue.

This is a robust and striking finding, and it speaks directly to how students come to know. As shown in Figure 2 (Panel A), the lower line represents those not assaulted. Their awareness of sexual assault being a problem on campus increases across the relational scale, moving from disagreeing with the statement on average (less than the scale's midpoint of 2.5) to agreeing. Notice that even among those assaulted since enrolling (top line), those who knew no one else in the community who had been assaulted were about as likely to agree as to disagree with the statement ($M = 2.5$). Thereafter, that line increases, also. While being personally assaulted since enrolling was not sufficient to believe sexual assault is a problem on campus (on average), knowing of others who had been assaulted was: knowing of another student on campus who had been assaulted was sufficient to see sexual assault as a community issue, especially if they had been told directly by a survivor. Knowing that others in the community have been assaulted is more informative about the nature of the community, on average, than being personally assaulted.[6] We can only imagine being a survivor within the community, disconnected from others' shared experiences, having to assume you are the only one. When asked if sexual assault is a problem on this campus, someone in that situation might well give the campus a pass. They might not link their assault to the campus, per se, whereas knowing they are not alone with the experience may implicate more starkly the local community itself. Similarly, even without personally experiencing assault, hearing from a friend who did may be enough to implicate the campus community more generally, especially if one were well connected to the whisper network within the undercommons and knew such experiences were commonplace.

Is this pattern unique to this particular institution, or does it represent other colleges and university student communities? We have closely examined the Association of American Universities' (2017) climate data to see if this finding generalizes to other universities. While the questions asked and how they were asked on the AAU survey differed from ours, they did ask students to rate the extent to which sexual assault or sexual misconduct is "problematic" at the (university). While their survey does not allow a duplication of our relational knowledge scale, it does allow an approximation. Rather than our trio of know no one, know of someone, and received a personal telling, the AAU survey permits responses of do not suspect other student(s) assaulted, do suspect other student(s) assaulted, and talked to student they suspected had been assaulted. We think this continuum, like ours, may register relational knowledge: a proxy for students' connectedness to other students' lived experience and whisper networks, their knowing-with. Further, these three AAU groups could be partitioned into those participants who had been assaulted personally and those who had not. As shown in Figure 2 (Panel B), our analyses of these six groups' agreement with the "sexual assault or sexual misconduct is problematic at [university]" statement produced a graph very similar to ours—similar enough to suggest our findings may indeed generalize to other colleges and universities. It may, in fact, be commonplace. It is striking how similar the graphs look. Students' knowledge that sexual assault is a local, community problem travels laterally and extensively by students telling students. Not all students know, nor does the college, but those who do know are affected, and their perception of the campus changes.

Our relational knowledge scale taps students' within-community connectedness and implies a knowledge of the community that runs more deeply than prevalence statistics can register.[7] It measures knowledge gleaned interpersonally through a connection with others, irrespective of one's direct experience with within-community sexual assault. It operates as an index of one's awareness of, proximity to, and susceptibility to this form of sexual violence within one's local community.

Compared to being unaware, coming into relational awareness of proximal sexual assault means one has discovered one's community is different than previously supposed and that other community members are different than previously imagined. This kind of knowledge is increasingly embodied the further up the scale one goes, such that one's relationship to the community varies across the scale, not abstractly or solely cognitively, but in an embodied and visceral manner, with a likelihood of eliciting shock, wariness, betrayal, fear, and anger. The portion of the community with whom one perceives oneself to be in communion, or potentially so, becomes increasingly restricted, even while one's connections, clarity, and agency within the whisper network become stronger. These steadfast differences in knowledge and awareness extending laterally, unevenly through the student community are manifestations of the sexual assault knowledge field.

These findings point to the social entwinements of physical, emotional, and cognitive upheavals that come from discovering your community is unsafe, that you and your friends are unsafe, and that some of your friends or acquaintances are dangerous. Because the findings are lateral, student generated, and at odds with the college's silence on the issue, they also present a register that the college itself does not share students' understanding—nor concern—at least not in the same way as students do.

Conclusion

We have described the relational knowledge field around sexual assault and identified some of the vertical and lateral informational gaps that persist within the college community. Viewing the institution's informational levies and channels from above, these knowledge gaps can be seen to reside within an epistemic field, where each gap relates to others. Most relational knowledge about sexual assault flows laterally, illicitly, student to student, through the undercommons. This pattern, as captured by the rule of thirds, shapes how students perceive the problematic nature of sexual assault. It is easier to remain relationally unaware, perhaps skeptical, as a student, if the college itself seems unaware. It is easier for the college to be relationally unaware if it simply counts officially reported incidents, and if their yearly tallies fall within "norms," and if the students who claim to have been sexually assaulted comply precisely with college policies concerning whom to notify and how, and especially, whom not to notify.

3

What One Needs to Know

Avoiders and the Cost
of Knowing

> When I first read the 1995 editions of
> *Hear My Voice*, I felt like each person
> who had contributed was sitting in my
> room with me. Each voice is so clear, so
> individual, so personal. Each voice is
> strong. Each demands their story be
> heard. Each reaches out and changes
> lives.
> —*Hear My Voice*[1]

Knowledge of within-community sexual assaults flows laterally, relationally, within, and by means of students' whisper networks. An important attitudinal shift seems to follow in its wake: knowers are more likely to say sexual assault is a problem at the college. Since sexual assault and sexual violence are problems on the campus, as they are at most campuses,[2] it is hard to escape the conclusion that those who know are savvier about the community, and those who don't know are relatively naive. In this chapter we explore the implications of this gap more fully: knowing versus not knowing. Focusing on the majority of students who have not personally experienced sexual violence since enrolling, we consider what it means for some to know and others not. Thereafter, we ask,

"Who are the not-knowers, and what comes with merely knowing?" A lot, it seems.

Epistemic Avoidance

What does it mean to occupy the category of not-knowing? We think of students who have not personally experienced sexual violence since enrolling and are yet unaware of others on campus who have as "avoiders," because they have somehow, and so far, managed to avoid encountering these uncomfortable features of the community and their peers' experiences. They are seemingly cut off from an important unsettling aspect of their immediate reality. Their ignorance might be active or passive and may be fleeting, but, consistently, a sizable portion of students fall into this category.[3]

How do we understand this kind of avoidance? Epistemic avoidance can take many forms. As noted earlier, everyone has blind spots or lacunae. Sometimes, this ignorance reflects limited experience or lack of curiosity about matters outside one's immediate social world. It is easy for members of privileged groups to avoid certain types of knowledge and to exist in a state of so-called ignorant bliss by not needing to know or by needing to not-know. The former, not needing to know, results from the oblivion that privilege and position induce—"I never had to think about it because it doesn't affect me." For many men and cisgender persons, for example, it is relatively easy to avoid seeing what many women and nonbinary people must contend with every day, personally and systemically.

Encounters with those with the privilege of not needing to know are hardly noteworthy. Not knowing allows those with privilege to move through the world with freedoms others cannot imagine, much less enact. Sometimes, a social media post, a conversation with a friend, a video, or a picture can disrupt the taken for granted. On occasion, those with privilege are exposed to these brief epistemic flashes. Emerald Fennell, the producer of *Promising Young Woman*, a film about a college sexual assault, describes a dinner party conversation in which one of her women friends shares her creepy encounter with a guy on the subway on her way to the dinner party. Following her telling, other women at the dinner party join in, sharing "one gruesome story after another," stories described as "too quotidian to be horrifying" (Chocano 2020). The men at the party were aghast, shocked. Disrupted by their tellings, one man confessed that he grew up thinking that everything was fine but now he was coming to the realization that "fine" applied only to him—his belated recognition of the gap, his own lacuna. Perhaps he glimpsed, also, his positioned susceptibility to gaps, his meta-blindness. Fennell surmises that men would not be so unaware if women were not culturally shamed into minimizing and normalizing their experiences to sustain the social imaginary, the "fairy tale in which everything was mostly fine and bad things only happened occasionally to girls who probably did something to deserve it" (Chocano 2020).

Friends, such as the men described above, may be unaware of their knowledge gaps. Their position as privileged group members shapes their relationship to this type of knowledge. Their avoidance is not deliberate or malevolent, necessarily, so much as it is a product of their limited opportunities to encounter contradictions, or what Medina (2013) refers to as "epistemic friction." Presumably, the men at the table had not yet encountered the double circumstance of needing to listen while being told directly by women about their everyday experiences. Once exposed to tellings or counternarratives from a friend, what had been previously avoided can be known and acknowledged relationally: felt, discerned, and experienced. Those who were heretofore unintentionally unaware can perceive themselves, their friends, and their community more clearly and realistically. They experience knowing-with. In this way, their relationships with their friends, their social world, and themselves as knowers can change profoundly, prompted by feeling shock and dismay.[4]

Other times, there can be a willful ignorance, an active avoidance of knowledge that is too uncomfortable, challenging, or disruptive to one's worldview, in which case one needs to not-know.[5] This, too, is a manifestation of privilege but also fear. Janet recalls an encounter with a neighbor inquiring about her sabbatical project. When she responded that she was writing a book about sexual assault, he responded, "Well, that's one book I don't need to read." The willfully ignorant actively avoid encountering knowledge that might change their worldview or might put them at risk somehow, and, should they encounter it, they might endeavor to bury it or deflect it in any number of ways—such as refusing to take it seriously, actively repudiating it and/or the messenger, or using their privileged position to apply some version of "catch-and-kill" to make the knowledge vanish, to name a few. Often, these repudiations manifest as credibility attacks: "You can't possibly know this to be true" or "This can't be true." The student researchers who approached Rick anticipated credibility attacks—hence their desire to conduct a survey and their need for support from a person with authority.

Judy Mann, a journalist for the *Washington Post*, tells a story about a radio interview in which she cites the statistic that one woman in four will be raped during their lifetime. She recounts that, within minutes, male listeners were calling to refute the statistic. One man claimed that since none of the women he knew well had been raped, one in four could not possibly be true. The male listener demonstrates an epistemological arrogance—if I do not know about it or it has not been part of my experience, it cannot be true—too common among those in privileged positions. This epistemic arrogance, its choicefulness, and the credibility attacks used to maintain it might explain why certain groups are not the first to know. The radio station host quickly replied, "Well, they are not going to tell you!" (Mann 1990, D3). In this way, "not telling some" and "some not knowing" become yoked, each one yielding the other—a dyadic driver of our epistemic triad, or rule of thirds

Mann's exchange highlights how knowledge about certain forms of personal experience is circulated, if at all, to selected audiences and how members of privileged groups can display epistemic arrogance toward stories and evidence that contradict or challenge their self-narratives. The privileged, prewrapped as they/ we often are within dominant ideologies and worldviews, can embody, too easily, the presumption of knowledge, of speaking authoritatively without suspicion or doubt. This arrogance affects the capacity to learn to self-correct and/ or be open to the corrections of others (Medina 2013). Similarly, racist and sexist ideologies skew relationships and information, warping and pitting the relevant epistemic fields. Such frameworks make all of us cognitively and affectively worse off, prone to and circumscribed by certain epistemic vices and virtues. The privileged are particularly susceptible to the vices of arrogance, laziness, and closemindedness. At the same time, marginalized groups, because of their oblique standpoints,[6] have easier access to the virtues of humility, curiosity, open-mindedness, and double consciousness. Medina (2013) adds that one's positionality does not dictate one's epistemic vices or virtues; rather, overcoming or avoiding one's vices and refining one's virtues require work, effort on behalf of the social participant to know oneself, others, and the world as part of the quest for a more just community.

Avoidance among students in the college community mirrors those we have considered more generally. When one matriculates into a small college community, one might well enter with an awareness and relational knowledge of sexual violence "out there" without yet knowing of its presence within one's new community, which is our principal interest. Entering students are almost certainly "avoiders," by our definition, having avoided, so far, being personally assaulted or otherwise victimized since enrolling, and not yet knowing of anyone else who has. This naive and circumstantial avoidance dissipates with time in the community as, unfortunately, some will be assaulted or otherwise sexually violated or intimidated, and some will eventually enter whisper networks where they will learn of others' experiences. Privileged students will never need to know, some will go out of their way to not know, and others will know but pretend not to.

The institution becomes a player in what is known and knowable and who is allowed to know and when and how. It is in the institution's interest to not know certain things that transpire, or if known, not to acknowledge, and, if necessary, to pretend not to know. They are, after all, legally responsible and liable, and because of federal, state, and local laws and policies, "to know" requires them to act. Like CEOs and presidents who might be purposively left out of the loop to eschew legal exposure, colleges must manage information flow. What is knowable up and down the institutional hierarchy and within the commons is governed, and it is partly governed by various needs to not know, or if knowing is given, to ensure what is known is in a form least destructive and costly to the school.

Needing to not know or to know as little as possible, as Medina (2013) describes, requires considerable effort to veil and ignore experiences and perspectives of those students who have been sexually assaulted or who have heard their stories and borne witness. The college is complicit in obscuring and limiting what most students know relationally. Until federal and state governments pushed for college climate surveys asking about sexual assault, campus leaders could claim near-total ignorance. Though colleges are now required to tally and adjudicate incidents of sexual violence and official allegations,[7] the knowledge acquired is truncated into propositions, and even very little of that, if any, is circulated in the commons. What the college "knows" officially is devoid of relationality, and what students know relationally is fenced. The institution, by policy, condones avoidance and the rule of thirds by minimizing opportunities for those with no awareness to encounter the kinds of personal, epistemic friction that foster understanding and the ensuing moral imperative for action. The institution minimizes what it "needs to know" by obscuring its complicity in the community's epistemic masquerade. The category of student avoiders is thus ensured, and what is known relationally circulates in secret.

We acknowledge that there are costs and benefits to knowing-with, and context and privilege help determine how one assesses their net value; within academic institutions, the perceived cost of knowing-with would seem to outweigh the perceived benefits, an epistemic stasis that favors avoidance. A social arrangement where knowledge and understanding are governed in this way by competing self-interests cannot possibly be epistemically just. An epistemically just community would eschew internal and external "resistances to knowing" and the unearned privilege of not knowing. Knowing and being open to knowing, having the capacity and the will to practice virtuous listening, and knowing-with are our shared moral and epistemic responsibilities (Medina 2013).

On the Cusp of Knowing

Students, especially new students, can be excused for not knowing—adults not as much. The data and testimonies are available. Much of what we will present in the next sections of this chapter probes what comes with knowing—that is, what comes when students know-with. A series of graphs and analyses have consistently revealed a pattern—that knowing with survivors changes students and how they perceive their community; hence it changes the community. Seeing this pattern revealed the significance of the episteme field. If seeing is believing, seeing has become our way of knowing about the field. We are reminded of how phone videos have been critical in documenting the racial violence that communities of color experience daily. Being asked to *see* reality firsthand directly confronts not knowing, one's resistance to knowing. Seeing it offers a direct challenge to the privileged, those who have not otherwise experienced it, to be less inclined to offer credibility attacks that discount or dismiss other people's reality.

Initially, we did not consider avoiders important to the epistemic field. Accustomed to focusing on survivors and their allies, avoiders showed up later in our understanding of the epistemic field. By including them in our relational knowing graphs as a methodological anchor, the power of relational knowing appeared—too obvious to ignore, too important to minimize. The avoiders point to possibilities for change. Our graphs expanded our thinking about the epistemic field, the impediments to knowing, and the importance of student whisper networks. Furthermore, they led us to ask, "What comes with knowing about this pattern of student knowing?" What will come of seeing the pattern?

Avoiders

Who are the avoiders? What do we know about them? How do they experience the college? The overall proportion of avoiders across all surveys since 2015 is 25.7 percent. As expected, the proportion declines with time in the community,[8] beginning at 36.8 percent among first-year students and declining to 16.7 percent among seniors.[9] The decline in avoiders across time in community represents students' increasing likelihoods of having been assaulted and knowing other students have. Setting aside the gravity of this "coming into awareness," the declining percentage of avoiders also registers students' increased capacity to perceive an aspect of the community that was initially obscured: that sexual assault is a problem on campus, and therefore that the community is fraught with risk and wounds.

Figure 3 depicts the relative percentages of avoiders by class and gender. Bar heights decrease from the first year to the senior year. As shown, avoidance within all groups diminishes with time in community, with the four-year decline among males (black bars) going from 42.3 to 21.1 percent and the decline among women and nonbinary students (gray bars) going from 31.3 to 12.2 percent. As one spends more time in a community and as one's social networks expand, there are increased opportunities to acquire knowledge about the experiences of others in the community. Rather than being fixed, students' epistemological status is in constant flux. Their awareness and attitudes toward the community can change dramatically across four years— like a river, always moving and changing, while the riverbanks and course hold firm.

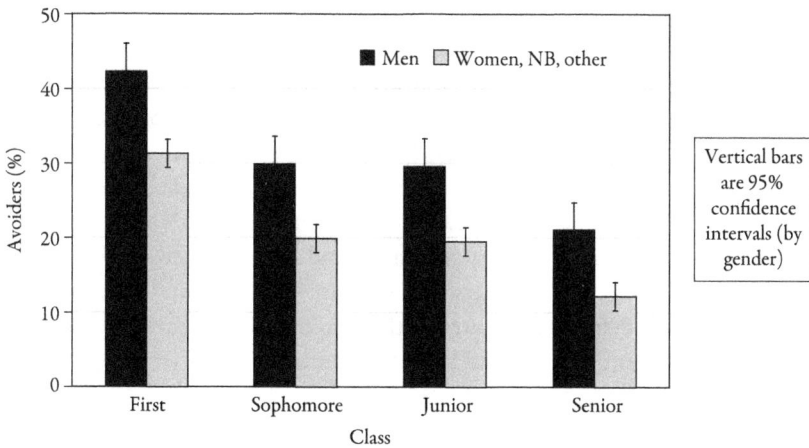

FIGURE 3 Percentage of avoiders, by class and gender.

Figure 3 points to other interesting findings: gender identity shapes what you may know about your community and your peers. Not surprisingly, students who identify as men are more susceptible to not needing to know or needing to not know. The black bars, representing men, are consistently higher than the gray bars, representing women and students who identify as nonbinary. As might have been expected, given our discussion of positionality and privilege, avoidance is more common among men than women and nonbinary students (Ms = 30.7 vs. 20.7 percent). That is part of the story represented by the bars in this graph.

The other part of the story, shown by the graph, points to possibilities for change. Notice how the black bars for sophomore and junior men are almost equivalent to the gray bars for first-year women. It is important to recognize and acknowledge how men, too, often change over time—in lockstep with their other-gendered peers. We must not lose track of this silver lining: people can change, and many do, often just from knowing-with.[10]

The proportions of students occupying the varying levels of awareness/experience along our knowing-with scale vary with gender and time in the college and of course with how we define the sexual infractions and knowledge that they have managed to avoid. In this case, it is avoidance of knowing or personally experiencing sexual violence of any sort since enrolling. Even though the rule of thirds is a heuristic, not a rule grounded in precise proportions, three sizable epistemically distinct student groups know and understand the community differently. In that sense, the triad is unchanging, akin to a photo snapshot, representing an epistemic triptych, a static institutional feature of student-community self-awareness.

What Comes with Knowing?

What are the implications of not knowing about sexual violence within one's community? Within the static, snapshot depictions presented by our biennial surveys, we have found that avoiders hold beliefs and attitudes at odds with those held by peers who possess knowledge of sexual violence.[11] Avoiders are more sanguine, more naive, less realistic, less skeptical about the community and its policies, resources, and responsiveness, and somewhat more likely to subscribe to gender-based entitlements. We summarize these findings, focusing on the costs and benefits associated with learning that others in the student community have experienced gender-based violence.

Less Regard for the College

We have already shown that knowers are more likely than avoiders to perceive sexual assault and violence as problems within their local community. Consider what else comes with seeing the problem up close as they do. In general, recognizing or perceiving a problem affects how one responds. Individuals are more likely to adjust their behaviors and mobilize others around issues they define as "problems" in their community, and that might be especially true when they encounter the problems personally. People who see climate change as a local threat, potentially affecting them personally, and know that it has already affected their neighbors, for example, are more likely to address the issue—to be more prepared for the next hurricane, for example, and support local policies as infrastructure initiatives. Shifts in perceptions are often, but not necessarily, the first steps individuals need to reassess and adjust their behavior and/or mobilize others.[12] By "perceiving the problem," we mean to suggest that the epistemic shifts involved are not exclusively propositional but instead include shifts in what one senses of one's reality, literally. Certainly, people were aware in 2020 that COVID-19 was a problem. However, their behaviors were shaped by their perceptions of its seriousness and their susceptibility, which were, in turn, shaped by what they experienced and witnessed in their immediate communities. In short, for change to happen within a campus community, it matters if sexual assault is perceived to be a problem.

Consider how students respond to statements that measure how they perceive the problem and institutional responses. Figure 4 shows the mean responses to these items and scales for each epistemic triad: avoiders, knowers, and survivors.[13] The leftmost cluster shows how students respond to the statement "sexual assault is a problem on this campus," by the epistemic category. The avoiders (white bar) disagree with the statement, whereas those who know (gray bar) agree with it. Comparing those who do not know of others versus those who do reveals what comes with knowing: an awareness that sexual assault is a campus problem. For context, the third bar (black) indicates that

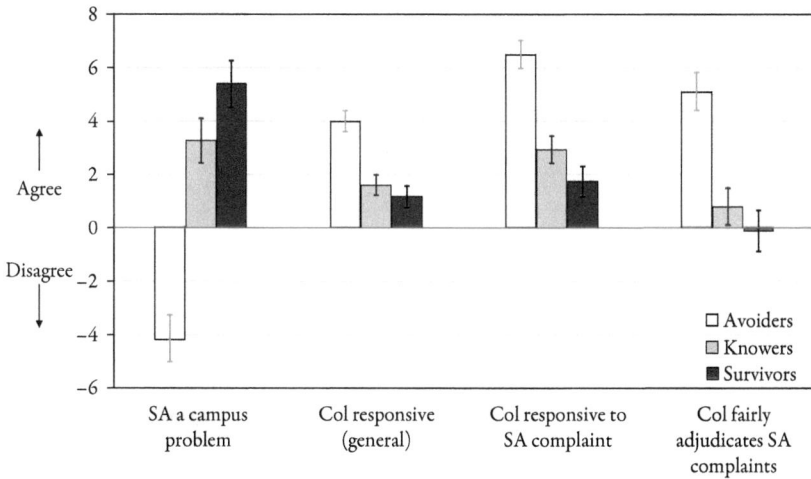

FIGURE 4 Regard for college, by sexual violence knowledge. What comes with knowing: agree/disagree that sexual assault is a problem on campus, or that the college is or would be responsive to their needs and reports.

those who know and have also personally experienced sexual violence agreed with the sentiment even more. We include the third bar to remind us of the obvious: that experiencing sexual violence is also an important factor in one's understanding that sexual assault is a campus problem. Our point is that merely knowing of others is sufficient to move the dial of awareness into this feature of the community.

The next clusters show the mean of our triad's agreement with three scales, respectively, left to right, students' sense of the college's responsiveness to their general needs, their sense that the college would be responsive to a sexual assault complaint, and their sense that the college would handle a sexual assault complaint fairly and responsibly.[14] Again, our focus is on those who have not experienced sexual violence since enrolling and, within that group, on those who *do not* versus those who *do* know of others who have, the first two bars, the white and gray bars, respectively, for each cluster in the figure. In each case, merely knowing of others is sufficient to decrease student confidence in the college. The avoiders view the college's responsiveness more favorably than those who know. Again, the third bar, the black bar to the right, which represents those who know and have also been subjected to sexual violence since enrolling, is included for context: they have even less confidence in the college, with mean ratings diminished to near the neutral point, and, for the item "would fairly adjudicate a sexual assault (SA) complaint," crossing the neutral point.

The AAU data (2017) offer an additional opportunity to test the generality of our findings. Their survey included a few items that tapped students' belief

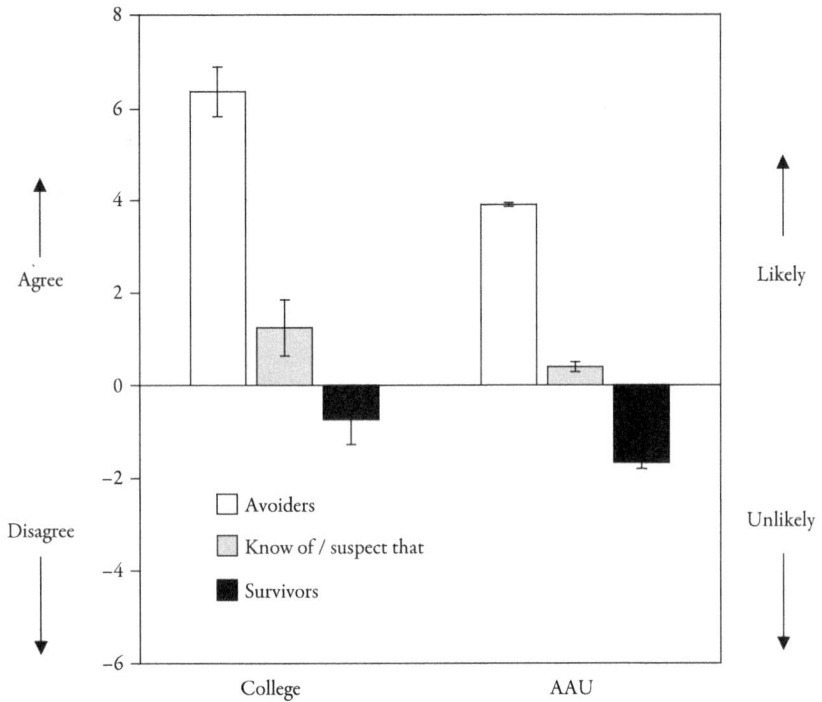

FIGURE 5 College/university responsiveness to reports, by data source. What comes with knowing: agree/disagree (on matched scale items) college/university would be responsive to reports of sexual assault or sexual misconduct.

that the university would be responsive to complaints of sexual misconduct. Five of them are conceptually similar to five of ours. We constructed matching five-item scales to compare the attitudinal shifts in responsiveness that "come with suspecting" (AAU) versus those that come with knowing. Results are shown in Figure 5. The three-bar cluster on the left is from our surveys, and the cluster on the right is from the AAU survey. Within the clusters, avoiders are the leftmost bars (white), knowers are in the middle (crosshatched), and survivors are to the right (black). The results from the AAU survey and ours are quite similar: those who know someone who has experienced sexual violence (or suspect someone who has) assess their college's or university's likely responsiveness to a report less favorably than avoiders, and nearly as unfavorably as survivors. Across many colleges and universities, what comes with knowing, in addition to perceiving that sexual violence is problematic within the community, is skepticism that the local leadership would respond well to official complaints. Our findings, in other words, are consistent with and hence representative of other colleges and universities, at least insofar as these sorts of attitudinal and epistemic shifts are concerned.[15]

One category of impact, one kind of cost of coming into knowing then, separate from personally experiencing sexual violence, is community-facing: the knower's relationship with the local community and with the issue of sexual assault being a problem within the community is different on average from that of the avoider. The consequence for avoiders who come into knowing is to see the community itself as problematic and to henceforth bring a realistic guardedness toward the college (or university) and some peers. By this reasoning, as students become more aware of their peers' experiences, including some within their social networks, they become more skeptical of the institution's ability to know what is happening to students in the undercommons and less trusting of the administration's ability to respond to a crisis, more generally, and to sexual violence specifically. With knowledge, students become aware of some of the epistemic inconsistencies and gradients within the community—what we are naming "gaps" and fractures—and they are confronted with the fact that their knowledge carries little agency within the institution. They can only whisper what they know to those primed to hear. In subsequent chapters, we will discuss the tellers and the secret keepers. While the knowers see the community more clearly—positives certainly—it should be clear that there are also often severe costs.

Rejection of Gender-Based Entitlement

Our surveys, but not the AAU survey, included questions about rape-myth adherence/resistance and attitudes about the college's consent policies, which define consent as ongoing, affirmative, and verbal. Overall, students at this college strongly reject rape myths and view verbal consent positively. However, avoiders, especially those who identify as men, are more susceptible to rape myths and less supportive of verbal consent principles. Results are shown in Figure 6. The left-hand panel shows the mean rejection of rape myth statements for our epistemic triad (avoiders, knowers, and survivors) separately for men and women (inclusive of nonbinary). While all six groups reject rape myths, on average, avoiders (white bars) do so less than knowers, especially those who identify as men. Similarly, in the graph to the right, all six groups view the college's ongoing verbal consent policies positively, yet avoiders view them less so, especially those who identify as men. Our focus, again, is on those who have not experienced sexual violence, comparing the avoiders with the knowers to get a sense of what comes from simply knowing with others, apart from what comes with sexual violence. The third bar (black) reminds us that those who are violated personally and know of others are also changed, usually more so. We saw in Figures 3 and 4 that knowing alone is sufficient to register attitudinal changes of a magnitude commensurate with those of survivors who also know, which is a key finding.

In this case, though (Figure 6), what comes with knowing is a lessening of one's susceptibility to gender-entitlement thinking and, presumably,

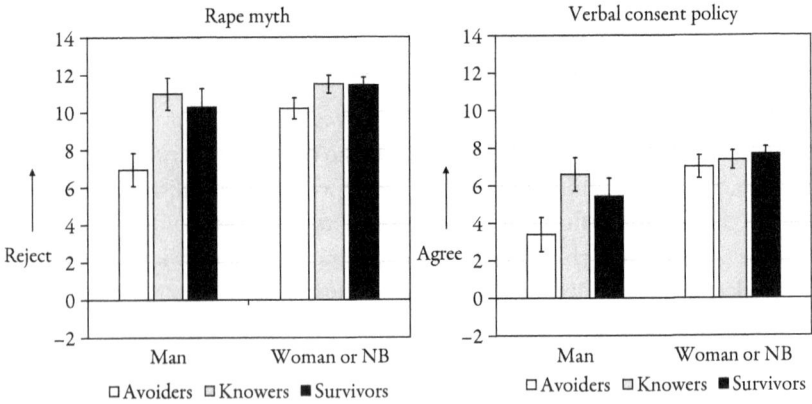

FIGURE 6 Gender entitlement beliefs, by sexual violence knowledge and gender. What comes with knowing: agree/disagree with rape myth statements and affirmative, verbal consent policies, by gender.

gender-entitlement action. Knowing-with seems to change people in this way, and on these issues, the change is most profound among men. Participating in the whisper network where knowing-with is mandatory seems sufficient to disrupt previously unexamined beliefs entrenched in the culture. People can change, and knowing with others may be the catalyst. These graphs reveal the epistemic fractures in the community. They also point to the epistemic possibilities within a community.[16]

We see these apparent consequences of knowing-with as positives. They lead us to posit various community intervention strategies we will return to later. But here, we want to emphasize that there are costs of knowing, of coming into knowing. Transformative change is painful and relationally challenging. It can be humbling and lead to shame and awkward interrelational hazards. Prior habits and friendships can be damaged or broken. Furthermore, in the face of knowing, people can be tempted to resist and to pull back to their former selves.[17] This is the "wanting to not know" that we spoke of earlier.

Again, students' awareness of within-community sexual assault can change and often does. When it does, attitudes change, becoming more realistic, less naive toward the college, and more consent-positive. Some of the costs of knowing, then, borne by students, are to see one's immediate community more realistically and to recognize one's own naivete and capacity to be fooled. Things are not what they seem. However, becoming more aware and discerning of one's community over four years is not guaranteed. Even among seniors, many avoiders hold attitudes and beliefs that are not much different from those held by students in their first year, nor much different, presumably, from those they held when they enrolled.

Our quantitative findings, replicated to the extent possible with the AAU survey data, show that avoiders and knowers view the community and the college/university differently. The data suggest ours is a representational story, which could extend to students beyond this college and the United States. We stand with students in Japan, Brazil, Mexico, and South Africa—everywhere the data have surfaced and students have shared their relational knowledge and asked, "What will it take to know more fully?"

What comes with knowing that other students have experienced sexual violence since enrolling is a heavier but more realistic view of the community and the institution's supportiveness. Avoiders are cut off from what knowers know and cut off also from the underlying source of what must seem like unfair critiques and attitudes toward the college held by their knowing peers. Additionally, based on our data, men who know are more likely to reject rape myths than their male avoider peers and are more likely to regard ongoing, verbal, affirmative consent policies favorably. Knowing-with, based upon these findings, changes people, instilling understanding, insight, awareness, and informed critique, much of it private, whispered, and when conveyed aloud, not understood, and often denied.

Personal Impact on Agency and Well-Being

I wouldn't be as actively involved in feminism if it were not for you. I also doubt that I would have the same career goals. I want to go to graduate school and get my master's in social work and work with victims of rape and educate the community on those issues. So, I guess I have grown from it, but I can't stop shaking. (Anonymous, *Hear My Voice*, 2005)

Since 2018, we have included numerous survey items that invited those who know of others and/or those who have any direct experience with sexual assault or sexual violence since enrolling to gauge the personal impact of their encounters. Sexual assault and sexual violence, more generally, are known to have seriously detrimental and sometimes long-lasting personal effects (e.g., Rothman et al. 2021; Cantor et al. 2017; Cantor et al. 2020). We set out to gauge the personal impact of sexual violence and the impact of simply knowing that others in the community have experienced sexual violence. Do the costs of becoming aware include detrimental psychological, behavioral, and/or academic changes? Similarly, it is well established that in the unfolding aftermath of and journey toward "recovery" from sexual violence, survivors often become more aware and engaged with the issue (cf. Strauss et al. 2021; Cantor et al. 2020).[18] We were also interested in whether that finding holds here. However, our primary focus was whether simply becoming aware of other survivors within the community is sufficient to induce this kind of community agency.

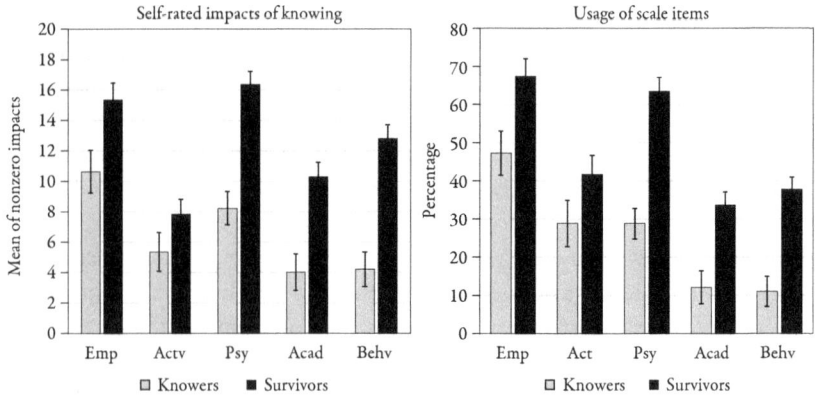

FIGURE 7 Self-assessed impacts on knowers and survivors. What comes with knowing: self-assessed impacts along five dimensions. Left panel: mean registered impacts. Right panel: mean percentage of scale items registering an impact.

Our surveys' impact items tap two positive dimensions of perceived change in oneself—greater empathy for survivors and more activism (action) around the issue of sexual violence—and three negative dimensions of perceived change in oneself—psychological, social/behavioral, and academic. The empathy and activism (action) scales were initially a single "activism" scale, but the results indicated two components: empathy and action. Changes in the action aspect of activism are less common than changes in empathy, and if they occur at all, they seem to depend upon or presuppose changes in empathy. Consequently, we consider these subscales separately.

Any nonzero impact registered by these items and scales is a cost or benefit borne because of coming into awareness of within-community sexual assault personally. The referent is the no-such-cost/benefit borne by the avoiders, who, by definition, without knowing or experiencing sexual violence, could not have experienced an impact thereof. To characterize what it means to be an avoider, we constantly reference impacts of knowing relative to zero, the absence of an impact, or the avoiders' privileged bliss.

Results are summarized in Figure 7, which has two panels. The left-hand panel shows, for each impact scale, the mean self-ratings by "knowers only," the gray bars, versus knowers who were also survivors, black bars.[19] The latter represents context, an anchor for evaluating the relative impact of those who merely know of others. The impact of those who merely know of others is our primary interest. A second anchor, also for context and comparison, is the x-axis itself, set at the "zero change" experienced by avoiders, by definition. Bar heights for the "knowers only" indicate ways in which knowers differ from avoiders and hence indirectly tell us something about the avoiders: they are not carrying these impacts, these "changes," whereas knowers are, and survivors even more so.

The right-hand panel shows the mean percentage of scale items that registered nonzero impacts to complement the mean ratings in the left-hand panel. For example, the psychological scale has nine items (see the appendix). The right-hand panel shows that survivors checked about two-thirds of the psychological items on average (about six), and the left-hand panel shows that the mean of those checked values was about 16. For context, if all students had checked "major change" for all their checked psychological items, the mean psychological impact would have maxed out at 30. With that framework in mind, based on these findings, what personal impacts come with knowing?

Relative to avoiders, knowers experience statistically significant positive empathic and activist (action) changes and negative psychological, academic, and behavioral changes. That is, their bar heights are significantly greater than zero. In each case, the impact on knowers is less than that experienced by survivors. Not shown here, but it is also the case that those experiencing the most severe forms of sexual violence report still greater impacts on each of these dimensions.[20] Clearly, sexual violence has profound consequences on students. Our findings indicate that just knowing others at the college who have experienced sexual violence since enrolling also has positive and negative consequences—less, on average, than those experienced by survivors, to be sure, but consequential even so.[21]

The patterns exhibited across the scales are also of interest. Whereas the empathic and activist changes that knowers experienced are comparable to those experienced by survivors (who also know), the same is not true for the other scaled impacts. The negative psychological impacts experienced by knowers are, relatively speaking, moderate compared to those of the survivors. The negative behavioral and academic impacts experienced by knowers are relatively minor compared to those of the survivors. One way to interpret these patterns is that hearing from others, or knowing-with, by its very nature may invite empathy and care. Otherwise, there might not be a telling, as empathy and care are requisite for telling. But for the telling to induce the kinds of changes tapped by the other three scales is likely a higher threshold, on average. Psychological changes, such as greater anxiety and others, perhaps can be understood to be intermediate, but for "hearing from others" to induce academic and/or behavioral changes of the sort included in those scales (e.g., missing classes, withdrawing from friends or activities, etc.) seems less likely. Certainly, it happens, and it is not hard to imagine scenarios where it would, such as being the close friend of a survivor of an alarming incident, perhaps inducing secondhand trauma. For instance, the peer accompanying their roommate to the emergency room for a sexual assault nurse examiner (SANE) exam might miss a class or assignment the next day.

Comparing the heights of the bars across the five scales is risky because we have no way of knowing if the scales are equally valid indices of their respective dimensions. It's tempting, for example, based upon the bar heights across the scales, to conclude that knowing of others evokes a greater change in empathy than it evokes in behavior or academics, but we cannot know that for sure from these data. We may not have asked the best questions to home in on behavioral and/or academic changes.

We can confidently say that these various self-ratings of impact experienced by knowers are another independent confirmation that being in communion with others' experiences, being relationally attuned to them, and knowing with them is epistemically powerful. It induces personal relational, affective, and behavioral changes. While many of these impacts are especially personal, the empathic and activist changes are not merely so; they orient toward others, community, and care. Accordingly, they are commensurate with those attitudinal and entitlement differences reviewed in Figures 3, 4, and 5. If empathy and activism are enhanced by knowing of others, then attitudes toward the college, the community, and gender-based entitlements might also be disturbed in tandem. The empathy evoked by relationally knowing of others' sexual violence experiences may be the epistemic friction required to trigger the moral imperative we mentioned earlier: for seeking to hold the college accountable, for staying active and communicative within the whisper network, for holding the survivors' stories, for acting on behalf of the issues.

Conclusion: The Power of Knowing *with* Students

How did these students, the knowers, come to know of other students' experiences? They were told firsthand or secondhand, and they listened. Moreover, they bore personal costs for being attuned to other people's troubles, but their gains were connection, knowledge, and agency. That knowing is sufficient to have predictable negative and positive consequences is the unsettling and bittersweet finding of importance here. It reveals more gaps with layers of complexity separating what avoiders and knowers do and do not know. That knowing induces complex personal dynamics, with positive and negative interactive components, across various items and dimensions is an invisible feature of the college/university campus and student community that is seldom noted. Its invisibleness and dynamism are particularly troublesome.

What has come from *our* knowing as researchers? The various kinds of impacts experienced by knowers redirected our attention to the unseeable: the roiling, layered community harm that exists in the wake of sexual assault and violence. Concern about the impact on individual survivors is warranted, and our findings suggest that the impact on survivors is certainly more significant, often much greater, on average, than the impact on knowers. However, the impact on knowers, those ready listeners, truly the unacknowledged first responders, is part of academe's tragic story and needs to be tended to and honored. The knowers and the not-yet-but-soon-to-be-knowers must not be overlooked in policy, research, and care. Their roles and burdens must not be obscured or diminished by the unimaginative nature of the questions asked or not asked. To do otherwise is unjust, an institutional and cultural betrayal.

In this chapter, we have explored and characterized more deeply what it means to occupy various sexual-violence awareness categories within the student community. We have shown that sexual violence is prevalent and consequential within the student community and that students tell one another, and we have shown that telling and listening to one another is consequential. Most students know someone within the community who has been sexually assaulted, and upward of a quarter have been personally assaulted. More students have directly experienced or heard of others who have experienced sexual violence more generally. Despite the prevalence of sexual violence and dyadic telling/listening/knowing, there remain many students who are seemingly unaware of and seemingly unaffected by this disturbance. Nevertheless, they must navigate the dynamics within the field. Those complex dynamics among students, of telling and not telling, of listening and not listening, of knowing and not knowing, with the college silent on the issue, produce an epistemic triptych—our persistent triad—and what we regard as an epistemically, experientially, fractured community. We remain amazed that so many students are unaware at any given time. We now recognize this as epistemic injustice, a deep, nearly invisible community self-wound.

In this chapter, we focused on those not told and who have not personally experienced assault, the avoiders, seemingly aloof or disconnected from the various whisper networks within the undercommons, contrasting them with those who know and what comes with their knowing. The avoiders perceive the community, the college, and their well-being differently, as if through rose-colored glasses. To all appearances, within the limits of our surveys, they have not been hurt, inspired, or in any way affected by the scourge. In the next chapter, we consider the primary source of knowledge within the epistemic field, the survivors who tell. What do we know about them, the various impediments that constrain them, and the resources that inspire them? What is their role in the knowledge field? Furthermore, why must they whisper?

4

The Secret Keepers

A sexual assault creates a peripeteia in a student's college experience, which explains why it rises to the level of awareness as something to be marked as out of the ordinary, even if it is not labeled as rape or assault.[1] Perhaps because it represents such a rupture of the ordinary, most students who have experienced sexual assault tell someone. As mentioned in chapter 1, over three-fourths of students who have experienced an assault tell someone, most often a friend, and most tell relatively soon after the experience, a finding reported in other studies of campus sexual assault (Banyard et al. 2010; Krebs et al. 2007; Hirsch and Khan 2020).[2] Studies show that women are more likely than men to tell, that persons with heightened feelings of distress are more likely to tell, and that feelings of self-blame decrease the likelihood of telling (Dworkin et al. 2016).

Telling someone is an action that brings the experience and the trauma into at least one relationship.[3] Hence, a critical distinction between secret keeping and silence holding—both strategies for managing concealed knowledge—is relational. Secret keeping invites others into the information management process. This action for the teller poses numerous risks: risks to self and identity (e.g., of shame, of being labeled as weak or "too" sexual), risks to relationships (e.g., of disrupting one's social circles, of hurting or overwhelming others), and risks to one's lived college experience and worldview (e.g., of assumptions about one's campus as a safe space, of one's right to sexual self-determination and autonomy, and of one's college plans and aspirations) (see Hirsch and Khan 2020).

Uncertainty permeates the telling encounter, and the myths associated with rape culture that place doubt, blame, and shame on survivors operate within the background as low-level cultural lighting. Can the survivor count on the friend to believe them and commit to entering the emotionally charged moment? Will the friend "be there" for them? Is it fair to ask them to bear witness? When is the best time to tell them, how can I explain it, and how can I begin? Telling is risky precisely because it introduces a dependency between survivor and confidant, speaker and audience. The survivor is no longer in control of the definition or meaning of the situation and/or the flow of information about identity and self. Survivors are often blamed for their assault and/or their interpretation of the incident is questioned. This questioning about one's judgment or interpretation of one's experience is often the basis for credibility attacks, the gaslighting that leads to epistemic injustice. Chanel Miller (2020) names some of the tactics used to discredit survivors and deter telling: "Society gave us one thousand reasons; do not speak if you lack evidence, if it happened too long ago, if you were drunk, if the man is powerful, if you will face blowback, if it threatens your safety" (327).

While tellings pose risks, they also hold the possibility of help, support, encouragement, understanding, and a way forward for the survivor. When a telling goes well, it offers the survivor and the confidant a chance to reaffirm the survivor's self-worth and relational competence and for both parties to co-construct knowledge around what happened. For the confidant, tellings hold deep meaning about the ethical obligations of friendship, empathy, and care, what it means to be trusted, and the safety of one's peer network and community.

Most tellings on campus move laterally following strong ties of association within the undercommons, rather than vertically through formal discursive channels such as Title IX, public safety, or other administrative offices. The students who belong to these rhizome-esque whisper networks, the survivors and their confidants, constitute over two-thirds (71.0 percent) of the student community. Almost half of the confidants in our surveys, 44 percent, have received tellings from two to three persons. These tellings are situated within an episodic temporal window with limited duration. Most confidants indicate they had talked about the experience with the survivor only once or a couple of times, and the survivor was most often the one who initiated follow-up conversations.

Persons in these networks of knowers, the secret keepers, have a lot to say, but as muted group theory suggests, they have little power to say it without getting into trouble (Burnett et al. 2009): trouble with survivors for violating their trust, trouble with administrators for failing to adhere to the proper administrative communication channels, and trouble with peers for disrupting social dynamics. If testimonial smothering (Dotson 2011) describes those who have not told others, we characterize secret keeping as a form of testimonial muting resulting from telling rules. The confidants are muted witnesses, the relational bystanders, to the sexual assault epidemic on college campuses.

In this chapter, we explore the whisper networks of both speaker and confidant to understand better the testimonial muting on campus. We listen closely and amplify what students have told us. What does it mean to hold this knowledge with someone else? What roles do friendship telling rules play in this process? Why is telling pervasive in the undercommons but mainly missing in formal discursive channels? As Lewis (2007, 13) points out, the "dominant group may hear nothing and assume silence, when in fact, members of the subordinate group are quietly whispering to one another." If speech about sexual violence cannot be silenced or excluded from discourse, then it needs to be muted and reduced to a whisper inaudible to those within the dominant discourse and to those who would rather not know.

Survivors: Sharing the Experience with Others

Telling introduces an opportunity to reconnect with someone who can be trusted after experiencing a fundamental relational breach, which can result in profound disconnection.[4] Sharing the experience presents an occasion to gain support, to practice talking about something very personal and difficult with someone else, and to engage in a shared meaning-making endeavor with others. Supportive relational contexts are needed for the construction of knowledge. Brison (2002) attributes her ability to make sense of her rape and to integrate it into her life narrative to a supportive relational milieu: "In order to construct self-narratives, we need not only the words with which to tell our stories, but also an audience able and willing to hear us and to understand our words as we intend them" (51). Survivors confide in close friends because relational norms that emphasize trust and concern for the well-being of a friend increase the likelihood the telling will be met with care and compassion. For most survivors, the sharing of their assault with a friend or peer is the only form of telling that occurs (at least at the time of our survey), and this shared knowledge becomes their guarded secret.[5] While telling poses risks, with trusted others it offers the potential to release some of the weight of the assault.

Releasing the Weight of Assault

In contrast to rational choice models of disclosure, survivors offer an explanation for telling a friend or peer about their experience that is more emotionally spontaneous and unplanned than cost-benefit models suggest. Bianca elaborates, "I had not planned on telling anyone, but it ended up being important for me emotionally to tell someone about that past for me and I hope others will be able to speak out. Even though my own experiences chain me from being able to share, others should have that space and should not have to feel afraid of being shamed, looked down on, or criticized over 'choices' they didn't even have in that moment. I told my partner about it because they are the first person I've felt comfortable enough to share something like that with." By putting "choice" in quotes, Bianca signals the contradiction between her experience and the language used to describe her action. She acknowledges how the fear of shame and judgment keeps survivors from speaking out. She also recognizes the emotional importance of sharing the experience with someone she feels comfortable with. Bianca feels chained to her experiences without an outlet for telling, and she hopes others can find a discursive space to tell without fear.

Other survivors describe the liberatory impact of sharing the emotional weight of the experience with others close to them. Kaitlin describes the positive impact of telling: "It really helped put me in the right direction to heal from the experience and helped to heal my scars and build me up stronger. When I finally told someone and subsequently went to seek help it helped me to feel that I truly was strong and that I was finally in control again. It was very freeing and it felt like the chains that were holding me captive were finally broken." Like Bianca, Kaitlin uses a chain metaphor to describe the "freeing" effects of sharing with others, a step in her "healing of the scars." Able to break free, she no longer felt captive to her assault.

Even with the hope of emotional support, survivors were quick to point out that telling was brutal: "Telling someone helped me get more support with my feelings and stress. But it didn't make talking about it or telling others easy." Other survivors share how "scared they were to tell people because I thought I had done something bad and I did not know how to talk about the situation." Jia explains that although it was "scary to divulge this information, choosing to do so was an affirming and empowering experience."

Of course, not all telling goes well; sometimes, telling is met with blame and disbelief, the effects of which can be devastating to the survivor. We need to make clear that we are not advocating for survivors to tell. We understand the risks associated with telling, and there are many reasons why one would not talk about an assault or would choose to omit certain details or resist labeling it as an assault. A survivor may limit what is shared if they are unsure of what happened and/or if they are unsure whether they can trust the hearer to listen and act without judgment. Alise, a student who was assaulted while studying abroad, reached out to a program coordinator to ask for help navigating a foreign health care system. Unsure of what transpired, she was concerned about how the program coordinator would react:

I was unsure if he was wearing a condom when he raped me and so this set off a lot of worry because I had to navigate a health care system in a different country to get tests and a prescription for PEP. I wasn't really sure whether I needed to take PEP. I was confused because I didn't know what had happened to me. I remember making google searches and I kept reading online "if you've been sexually assaulted get tested for STIs and take PEP" and I kept asking myself subconsciously "was I sexually assaulted?" It's been hard for me to name what happened. I've only been able to call it what it is (rape) in writing. I've never described it as rape out loud to anyone. However, I didn't feel like I could tell my program coordinator (who helped me access medical care) that it was rape. Instead I told her I just had sex with someone without a condom and I felt that she was annoyed by the whole predicament. Getting the tests and interacting with my program coordinator really SUCKED. . . . I decided I should probably go see a counselor and went to the health center where I got good support. Since going to therapy, I've told a couple more friends. I'm not sure if I'll ever tell my family.

The program coordinator was not someone Alise thought she could trust to listen and not judge her. Sensing the coordinator's annoyance, Alise omitted details of her experience to get the information she needed to secure health care. In time, with support from others, Alise has told a few friends and her therapist, though she admits she is unsure if she will ever tell her family. Some tellings are too risky to self; some are too hard for others to hear.

When others fail to respond as expected, the survivor may question their interpretation or definition of the situation and may reassess telling. A reaction to a telling influences whether the survivor feels empowered to continue sharing with others or is deterred from future tellings. For one survivor, the absence of a compassionate reaction from a close friend threatened the meaning the survivor had assigned to the incident: "Receiving almost no reaction from telling someone very close to me made me question whether or not anything had actually happened to me, which made me worry about telling others." For Dan, his friend's judgmental reaction intensified his feelings of shame and blame:

> It made me reluctant to tell other people what happened and mostly I felt ashamed, guilty, anxious, and angry. I was angry with her for not understanding and angry at myself for getting drunk and going home with a guy I just met. I felt uncertain about what to do. I wanted to go get PEP because he didn't use a condom, but I felt too embarrassed about the circumstances (me being drunk, us both being men, it being a one night stand, etc.) so I didn't want to explain what happened to a nurse to get the PEP so I just didn't go. Her judgmental reaction worsened my anxiety, made me more afraid to seek medical care, stopped me from telling other people about it, and left me feeling deeply ashamed and embarrassed, like it was my fault.

Tellings are often a way to check if others share the same perspective, to gauge whether they also agree the "behavior was not normal or appropriate."

It is a way to practice how one talks about it with others. There aren't many opportunities for young adults to learn how to talk about sexual experiences, in general, even less so when the experience is negative or traumatic. The reaction to Dan's telling, the judgmental reaction of his friend, intensified the effect's impact, and consequently, he shut down. Questions that challenge motive, decision-making, and/or the sequence of events alter the structure of a telling, a point we will discuss in chapter 6 regarding Title IX procedures. When a telling of assault is questioned, intentionally through disbelief or credibility or unintentionally due to ignorance, the possibility of epistemic injustice increases.

Understanding the aftermath of an assault is about more than understanding what happened (Hirsch and Khan 2020; Germain 2016). The aftermath requires these experiences to be rendered meaningful. Telling is also about creating a shared understanding of the incident. This meaning-making process is a vital part of what makes the meaning of the experience, co-constructed with others through connection, real. Survivors and confidants coproduce knowledge as they work to make sense of the situation. Telling others moves the experience into a shared discursive realm that makes it "real" because the definition of what occurred is no longer completely in the survivor's control. Kamala explains, "It helped release a weight off my shoulders, but it made the situation more real."

Making It Real

Bringing others "into the know" makes ignoring or minimizing the experience harder. Sharing what happened with others is key to understanding what happened, even if the "it" goes unnamed. The label may emerge as part of the unfolding narrative over time. Mia admits, "Telling a peer helped me realize how awful what happened was and that my feelings were real. It helped me process and approach my perpetrator and helped me feel empowered about my sexual voice." Aaliyah names her confusion and how her friend helped her process the experience: "I wasn't harmed by the incident, just confused. So I told a friend to help me understand what had happened and why because it just didn't make sense to me." Other survivors point out how the conversation with a friend helped them (re)frame the severity of what had happened while validating their sense that something "wrong" had occurred. Grace, who shared her experience late at night with friends, realized the significance of what had happened after telling: "They were great about supporting me and making sure I was okay, but I hadn't realized it was a big deal until I said it out loud." Saying it out loud makes it real and marks the beginning of an account that may birth a more substantial narrative over time. Sometimes, friends can name what survivors cannot voice or utter aloud.

Aware of how others might interpret the incident, some survivors struggle to maintain control over defining their experience. Some survivors resist the label of assault because the experience does not match the perceived level of severity the term evokes. Hirsch and Khan (2020) found in their ethnographic study that students exchange "war stories" about assaults, which can have the effect of silencing students who think their story does not match the intensity or severity of others they have heard. Struggling with how others might label the incident, Maddie describes her inner turmoil over the "severity" of her experience: "I debate a lot with myself about how serious it really was and how serious others will make it even though it's not really for me. I sometimes don't feel like talking about it because I feel people will make a huge deal out of it in a way that does not represent my experience and perception, and sometimes I feel like talking because I kind of realize that it was important. I think culture and cultural differences play an important role in that confusion." Maddie attributes her confusion to a mismatch between cultural definitions and her experience. Lacking the hermeneutical resources to align cultural definitions with experience, Maddie identifies the gap between experience and the language needed to describe what happened to her. She worries that others will assign a meaning to her experience that she doesn't share. Consequently, although she feels like talking, her fear that others will misrepresent her experience mutes her testimony.

Friends often offer an alternative perspective. Emma describes how her friend's validation provided a narrative frame through which she could process the experience and talk about it more comfortably: "My friend said that it was assault and that validated my experience. On one hand I felt like the incident wasn't that bad but still felt like it was affecting me significantly. By telling my friend and hearing her support, I felt more comfortable to talk to others about it." Like many others, Emma did not feel like the assault was that "bad," even though it was significantly affecting her. Her friend's ability to listen and name what had happened helped her move forward.

Other survivors describe how talking about the experience with friends "validated their reaction" and helped them "understand that the action still wasn't okay." For a few, the confidant's response deepened their resolve to tell others, even when it made them "uncomfortable." Noting how her telling was "well received," Autumn explains, "a lot of times people don't think women can be assaulted by other women, but it happens all the time. It made me want to tell more people about it." The reaction of her friends to her telling empowered Autumn to share her experience with others to disrupt gendered stereotypes.

In this next section, we turn our attention to the confidants. How do they make sense of what they have heard? How do they react in the moment? How do they process the assault? What implicit and explicit norms govern how they manage this acquired knowledge?

The Social Network of Friends and Peers

Studies exploring the impact of a telling on friends and social networks (Kirkner et al. 2018; O'Callaghan et al. 2021) find that sexual assault is a shared crisis, a peripeteia, to both survivors and those around them. Confidants describe feeling scared, surprised, confused, shocked and upset, sad, empathetic, calm, angry, and "like they needed to throw up." Specific details of the telling leave a sticky imprint in their memories. When asked to describe what stood out to them about the telling, confidants describe the survivor's emotional/affective response: "the self-blame," "her expression and reaction when telling the story," "how calm she was," or "how she sobbed," how "scared," "the crying behind the door of the bathroom stall," or how "unemotional the person was in describing the experience." The range of reactions serves as an important reminder of the need for trauma-informed education that teaches the community about the myriad reactions to sexual violence and the importance of not assuming everyone responds similarly. The confidants' reactions serve as a reminder of how an assault's aftershocks vibrate through a community, extending beyond the survivor. Jessica, a senior who had received three disclosures while enrolled at the college, explains, "It was very disturbing to hear in all disclosures. One person was only eleven years old when it happened to her and never had told her parents. Someone else had to take time off from COLLEGE since seeing the person who raped her on campus did not allow her to feel safe and impacted her mental state dramatically. The other person told me and others in a classroom setting. It was the first time I heard someone at COLLEGE disclose that they were raped. All disclosures were very different from each other." Like many confidants in our surveys, Jessica had received multiple tellings while enrolled at college. Each telling, though quite different, was deeply disturbing. Certainly, these incidents and their tellings constitute peripeteias for those involved. At any moment, student networks may be holding multiple tellings of assault at any given time. As Hirsch and Khan (2020) found in their research, some peer groups have become so emotionally oversaturated with assault stories that individuals do not feel comfortable talking about their own experiences anymore.

For students who have received multiple tellings, imagine how they might respond to an institution's claim that sexual assaults are infrequent (and assaults seem infrequent if you use official reports and Clery statistics as *the* source of knowledge). They might wonder if the administrators are members of the same college community—perhaps the brick-and-mortar campus, but certainly not the epistemological community. One might ask how they could not know given the ways, as Jessica's account suggests, assaults seep into the community: as a retention issue, as an emotionally charged moment in the classroom, and/or as part of the unseen burdens students bring with them to college. As Alcoff (2018) describes, "Sexual violations transform us. Both victims and perpetrators are transformed, as well as their families, friends, and social circles. Just the knowledge that such events are real possibilities in one's life, however remote, has an impact even on those who have had no direct experience of them" (94).

They Knew They Could Trust Me

Individuals learn how to handle different types of information and, for each type, who its appropriate recipients are. Children and young adults learn what information to share with parents versus friends. Employees learn the appropriate communication channels for disclosing a work problem. In his work on notification norms, Ryan (2006) discusses the expectations around who is "the first to know" and how violations of those expectations can damage relationships. People understand that one shares hard things to those with whom they are close. People are more likely to confide in others with whom they feel emotionally connected. The very definition of closeness depends on the nature of what is disclosed and how one manages this information. Close friends are expected to share secrets and keep their secrets safe. Even young children understand this friendship rule and how "letting the cat out of the bag" can damage a friendship (Liberman 2020).

Adherence to the telling rules of friendship, particularly among those with close ties, carries a relational obligation, a moral duty of sorts. Will the confidant keep their secret? Will the confidant's actions, particularly toward the perpetrator, reflect this newfound knowledge?

Survivors expect their friends to engage in virtuous listening, meaning they expect trust, support, emotional attunement, and presence. Francisco (2000) describes this as listening infused with love and anger. Most students understand "how to hear" a story of assault. Of students who have received a telling, their overwhelming response to the survivor was to listen (73 percent) and to assure the survivor they were not to blame (58 percent).

Confidants understand the obligation that accompanies a telling and trust's role in fulfilling one's responsibility to the other. Friends are predisposed to trust each other and, as Aristotle (quoted in Crisp 2014) writes, to take up the other's good as their own. Some philosophers claim that friendship demands epistemic partiality (Stroud 2006); people are more willing to interpret the behavior of a friend more positively, to extend to a friend the benefit of the doubt. Testimonies from friends carry more significance than those from strangers (Hawley 2017), hence the power of "knowing-with" over "knowing-of." Conditions that foster trust may be easier in intimate relationships than in institutions.

Trust is the ground on which the seeds of a telling are sown. For a telling to take root and become relational knowledge, it requires trust. Not surprisingly, trust is a frequent theme in response to the question, "Why did they tell you?"

Eva acknowledges, "I was close to the person, and they felt they could trust me." Other confidants emphasize the role of trust:

- "I was someone this person decided to trust."
- "Because they trust me and couldn't hold it in."
- "They were fairly close to me, so I assume they trusted me."
- "They needed to talk it out with someone they trusted, get it out of their mind."
- "I feel that I was trusted enough to be a good listener, and to believe their story unconditionally."
- "They trusted me to listen, understand, and not look at them differently."
- "I felt that this person trusted me with their story and that I would never use this information against them. Through our friendship and through student employment roles on campus, we had built mutual trust and care. I would do whatever I could to support them, follow their wishes, and ask what they needed."

Tellings are critical sources of knowledge *if* there is trust (Dormandy 2020; Pohlhaus 2017; Hawley 2017). Trusting someone to believe what they say and trusting someone to act are epistemologically fundamental to knowledge creation. When someone offers information to another and that person trusts what they say, if all goes well the person gains testimonial knowledge (Hawley 2017). For the confidant or hearer, trusting the survivor involves a belief that they know what they are talking about, what philosophers refer to as competence, and that they are sincere (Fricker 2007; Hawley 2017), meaning they are not trying to deceive or mislead the confidant.

When students approached Rick about developing a survey that would measure the extent of sexual assault on campus, they weren't simply looking for someone with specific research skills; they were looking for someone they could trust to hear what they had to say. By virtue of his position, he had more power than the students to shape their narrative about campus sexual assault. However, Rick had demonstrated to students a quality essential to relational knowing: trustworthiness. Students and colleagues sought him out as a confidant because they perceived him as trustworthy, someone who could be counted on to engage in virtuous listening during the toughest of conversations. He could be trusted to take up the work with compassion and competence. After all, trust is one part affect, one part cognition.

When a survivor shares an experience, it signals to the hearer that the survivor believes they are someone who can be trusted with this information. The shared commitments of friendship offer the possibility of strong trust relations that allow both parties to take risks (Grasswick 2018). Tyesha elaborates,

"I believed them and understood that it took a lot of courage to open up about their experiences. I recognized that disclosing their experience with me meant they felt safe and comfortable with me. Finally, that I should respect their privacy and keep it to myself." Tyesha understands the risks involved and the courage it takes to tell someone about this kind of experience. She also understands that because the survivor told her, and not someone else, this conveys something about the nature of their relationship. She is someone who can be trusted, someone who is "safe." As a "safe" friend, she implicitly agrees to respect her friend's privacy. Confidants understand the telling/hearing rules at play: listen, believe the survivor's story, follow the survivor's lead, and protect the secret.

Measuring the aftershocks of an assault extends beyond just understanding what happened but also understanding how meaning is constructed by friends (Hirsch and Khan 2020). Some confidants can articulate how trust creates an epistemic opening, inviting them into the telling as a meaningful co-collaborator, as someone who helps the survivor process the incident. Lee writes, "They knew they could trust me with the information, and they needed help processing what had happened to them." Nari shares, "They were trying to understand what all happened to them and came to me for help and advice." Others, like Jada, share how trust and vulnerability, a potent combination, create the relational and epistemological space for a friend to open up about their assault. Jada explains,

> She and I had a really close relationship. She's a sex worker and was raped by three men at gun point. One night, after a trans support group, she pulled me aside and started crying and told me everything. She hadn't told anyone in the three months since it had happened. I believe she told me because she needed to share it with someone, I had just been vulnerable in the group, and she trusted me. I can't speak for her. I don't know exactly why she chose that night to disclose, but I believe it was a combination of her trust in me and my preceding vulnerability/opening up. I think she also just reached a breaking point and needed to say it.

After keeping silent about her rape for three months, Jada's friend needed a safe space to share what had happened to her. Trusting Jada and following her lead, her friend was able to step into this emotional clearing and disclose what she had been carrying with her for months.

Navigating the Social Dynamics of the Peer Network

Although many survivors know the person who assaulted them, the effects of an assault on the peer group are understudied. As Hirsch and Khan's (2020) research shows, peer groups are an important element in the dynamics of sexual assaults on college campuses, in terms of both creating opportunities for sexual encounters and processing the aftermath of an encounter. Students are aware of how an assault, often involving someone in their social network, can fracture one's social circle. When it is a friend or partner who commits the rape or assault, the survivor weighs the impact of defining the experience as an assault on their identity and the impact of defining someone within one's social circle as a rapist or assaulter. Does the survivor want to "ruin" someone's life, someone they know? The perpetrator's connection to the social circle is a consideration before telling because of its perceived impact on the network (Dworkin et al. 2016), specifically the relational effects and safety concerns for others in the network who could be at risk.

Our multivariate modeling of who tells revealed the importance of the social network. The survivor's perception of the support for the accused was a significant predictor of telling. Those who perceived support for the perpetrator were less likely to tell, and this factor was significant even after controlling for incident characteristics, such as type of assault, extent of coercion or force, and the perceived support for the survivor. In recounting an incident that involved someone from her hometown, Jaelyn shares, "It made me feel more comfortable telling others. I was worried about the social backlash of the situation. The person who made me feel uncomfortable is very well liked among my group of friends from home and I was unsure if anyone would believe me. I also did not want to make all of his friends hate him, but I wanted him and others to know that he was acting in an inappropriate way. By receiving the support I did from my then boyfriend, I felt that people would believe me and support me." Jaelyn names the social risks that come with telling and how, within social circles, telling can test friendship loyalties. Whom do you believe? Jaelyn expresses concern for the person "who made her feel uncomfortable." She doesn't want others to hate the person, but by telling she also wants to mark the incident, to him and his friends, as inappropriate. The support of her former boyfriend, and perhaps his social capital within the group, provided her with the credibility she needed to tell others.

Social dynamics within the peer network introduce additional layers of complexity to telling. Amaia regrets her decision to tell her friends because it negatively affected her social networks:

Telling my friends was an enormous mistake, as this school is so very small and people use any possible dramatic information as social ammo, and it spreads like wild fire. Many people were more concerned with the perpetrator's social capitol/other social relationships and history, that how I was feeling/how I wanted to move forward with the trauma was entirely trampled over. Many people, some of whom I didn't even know well, found out/told each other and even came to me begging for emotional support surrounding THEIR experiences with the perpetrator. Many people tried to force me to relay my experience to them in detail so they could judge its validity. Many people tried to control what actions/steps I took to take care of myself, and refused to respect my boundaries/processing time and lectured me about how I wasn't taking care of myself. I felt constantly blamed and disempowered, and like I was a catalyst for drama and pain no matter how much I tried to hide what happened and protect my privacy. I felt I had to choose between privacy and utter loneliness, or complete alienation. The perpetrator himself ended up feeling like the only person I could really talk to—He was the one who remembered what happened. He held so much power, and he very easily manipulated me into expending all of my energy to protect him (the only person who seemed to "understand" me) than expend energy actually figuring out what I needed or wanted. And when he eventually felt in the clear and people got bored and stopped being interested, he stopped talking to me all together. And I was left still trying to figure out healing alone. I felt abandoned. And it feels like I did it to myself.

Amaia's account illustrates how survivors are often expected to manage network dynamics, including interpersonal dynamics and the flow of information. Negative information can travel fast within networks, and friends can weaponize it to disparage members of the group. Amaia's friends blamed her for the social rupture and the pain she was inflicting on the group. She also found herself in the position of caring for others who sought support from her over their own assaults. In a paradoxical and manipulative way, her assailant turned out to be the person she could talk to about the incident, which ended when he "felt he was in the clear." Amaia's experience illustrates what some may experience as a Faustian dilemma of sorts: tell and implode one's social networks only to be socially isolated or keep the experience to oneself and risk self-alienation.

Knowing how to handle a telling in the moment is one thing; knowing how to handle it over time presents new challenges. How is the friend expected to interact with the perpetrator after receiving a telling? How long do confidants need to "be there" for the survivor? Trust carries expectations for action, and when a friend fails to meet these expectations, the survivor can feel betrayed. Tasha told only a few close friends because she did not want the word to get out. As a survivor of multiple assaults, she understood how friends struggle to know how to handle this information: "After telling one or two people I decided not to tell anyone else because information spreads FAST. My close friends are good at responding in the moment but don't know how to handle it as time goes on. Usually after telling friends they either decide to 'cancel' the perpetrator or just move on as if nothing had happened." The former, instead of the latter, appears to be what survivors count on. Isabella explains, "Telling people about this situation made me feel hesitant to discuss it with others because although they seemed supportive of me, they continued engaging with the person who assaulted me as if nothing had ever happened." Though her friends provided support, Isabella also expected them to act differently toward the person who assaulted her based on this newly acquired knowledge. When her friends continued to interact with the person who assaulted her, Isabella felt betrayed.

Though telling others can elicit support and offer a way to process the experience and make sense of it, efforts to reduce the discomfort can backfire. Hannah describes how the initial reaction to her telling felt supportive, but her friends' efforts to make her feel better, to relieve her discomfort, only made the situation worse: "I felt okay talking about it at first, it was only through talking about it that I realize that the experience was non-consensual in some ways. I felt supported when talking about it, but the efforts of other people made light of the situation to try and ease my discomfort but that has made the bad experiences worse." Though her friends' actions may have been attempts to ease her discomfort, making "light of the situation" seemed to discredit her experience. Support needs shared understandings and meanings to be felt and sustained.

Not My Story to Tell

A student pokes her head into Janet's office to say hello. Since taking Janet's class last year, she has continued a series of informal conversations about her academic interests and how her classes are going. The student asks about the research project, and Janet begins to update her on what she is thinking through at the moment, which happens to be this chapter. As Janet describes the role of friends, she notices a change in the student's facial expression: her face becomes red, and her eyes fill with tears. Janet stops midsentence and says, "I can see what I am describing resonates with you." The student admits she has her own story, adding it occurred prior to college. Janet listens. The student quickly redirects the conversation back to questions about our project, a rhetorical move Janet suspects is intended to lessen her discomfort. Janet follows her discursive lead. Regaining her composure, the student shares a story about a friend of a friend who was assaulted and how the alleged perpetrator is in her class. She felt compelled to share her knowledge about the situation with the faculty member even though she felt conflicted about sharing something so personal outside of the social network. She asks, "Did I do the right thing?" Knowing the right course of action is not easy, particularly when one encounters conflicting telling norms.

Relationships are built on trust, and most confidants keep the secret as a way of honoring the trust placed in them and of protecting the friend's identity and reputation. In contrast to those who have experienced an assault, the majority of those who receive a telling, 68 percent, do not tell anyone else about the assault. Of the respondents who elaborated on why they chose not to talk about the telling with anyone else in the 2020 climate survey, a large percentage (46 percent) said "it wasn't their place," "their story to tell," or "none of their business," an indication of the power of telling rules. Jess, a queer survivor who has not shared her friend's telling with anyone, names the normative violation: "That would be shitty. If they are uncomfortable going further I respect that, the system is terrible and I understand not wanting to fall victim to both a sexual predator and systemic victim blaming." To violate a friend's trust is "shitty," something one would not do without a compelling reason. And perhaps because of their own experience with sexual violence, Jess recognizes that it takes time to sort out what happened.

Friends are reluctant to shortcut the meaning-making process and to usurp the survivor's agency in determining how they want to proceed. Rachel explains, "It's her process and healing to decide the publicity of this moment in her life. We are really close friends and I know that I could encourage her to mention it to the administration, but it doesn't feel like my place if she was not super comfortable with that." Chris, a first-year student who identifies as nonbinary, echoes this sentiment: "I didn't want to usurp their agency in determining the best way for them to talk about and deal with the experience." Most understood the need to give the survivor the time and space to process the experience and decide how they wanted to proceed. Sharing the information with others, particularly college officials, usurps the survivor's agency.

The trust and loyalty associated with friendship keep the secret safe and protected from the potential harm that exposure brings. Though some survivors explicitly ask their confidants to keep the secret—about a quarter of the confidants in 2020 indicated they had not told anyone because the survivor "asked them not to"—most confidants understand this to be an expectation, implied due to the nature of the telling. Derek makes it clear that he didn't plan to violate the survivor's privacy, but that he did make it clear that he could be counted on for further help: "I did not feel the need to and did not want to violate the survivor's privacy. The survivor made it clear she did not want any assistance and did not need to discuss it further. I made it clear that I was there to help in any way I could if she needed." As Derek indicates, protecting the privacy of the survivor is a relational obligation that is closely entwined with the sense that some stories should be shared only by their author.

To break the trust of a friend jeopardizes the relationship, and our research shows that confidants break the trust placed in them only if they need help dealing with the impact of the telling on their own emotional well-being and/or they are concerned about the safety of the survivor or others in the network. In all, 32 percent tell someone about the incident, but in ways they believe minimize risk to the survivor. Cy, a queer nonbinary student, was confused when someone who had previously assaulted them confided in them. This additional complexity prompted Cy to reach out to a friend, but in a way that didn't violate the survivor's trust. Cy elaborates, "HIS assaulter turned out to be a friend of mine. I told a close, trusted friend from a different friend group as to not cause unwanted-drama or betray the victim (my assaulter's) trust. I told them within the week." Even when circumstances call into question the norms of obligation, Cy takes care not to betray the trust of the survivor.

Most confidants turn to friends outside of their college network and/or to parents or therapists for advice or support to avoid violating telling rules. Confidants describe feeling "so overwhelmed or distraught" that they need to process the experience with someone else. Even when the relationship between survivor and confidant is less intimate, carrying this knowledge is a lot to process. Evan, who admits that he wasn't a particularly close friend to the confidant, sought the support of a friend back home: "I told a friend from back home (not a THIS COLLEGE student, one who has never met the friend who disclosed) about a week after the disclosure. I felt I needed to tell someone because it was a lot to process, and I trust the friend I told." To mitigate the effects of breaking a telling rule, Evan looked outside of the college community, a tactic that protected the survivor while providing support for his own emotional well-being.

Feeling particularly overwhelmed, Dylan needed an outlet to process his feelings about learning that his brother was assaulted: "I have a girlfriend who I have dated for six years. She is also a good friend with my brother, and she is phenomenal at keeping secrets. I needed an outlet, because I felt like I was going to crumble at any minute. That's my brother. You never expect this kind of thing to happen to your brother, especially when his assailant was a woman." Dylan needed someone who could help him process his brother's assault and the reversal in stereotypical gender expectations about who can be assaulted and by whom. He selected someone who was a phenomenal secret keeper.

Confidants are more likely to tell parents, particularly mothers, and therapists, within a shorter time frame than survivors. As discussed earlier, the minority of survivors who do tell parents tend to do so after some time has passed, a finding we suspect reflects a desire to not worry parents and/or to assure them, when they tell them, that they are okay. For confidants, on the other hand, talking to parents about someone else's assault engages a support strategy that isn't as emotionally taxing to the parent since it involves an oft-unidentified friend. Marisa, a Latinx student who knows both the survivor and the assailant, describes the anger she felt when her friend told her about her experience. She shares that she "told my mother that evening, because it was scary, and I needed to talk about it with someone I trust." Marisa needed to process her emotions with her mother, and she needed to share the experience with someone she trusted.

Cara also turned to her family and her therapist for advice about how best to support her friend: "After the disclosure, I was disturbed and deeply worried about my friend. I turned to my personal therapist and my family for advice about how to best support my friend within the next week." Like Cara, Julie turned to her family and therapist to help her process the telling. But Julie's own experience of assault by someone who threatened to harm her if she disclosed it shapes her understanding of the telling. When asked why she shared the telling with others, she explains, "I told a friend at home because I needed to talk it out, also they were open about their experience on campus and wanted people to know what happened and who that was, told a therapist as well, told my parents within twenty-four hours." In her account, Julie reminds us that she hasn't violated the trust of her friend since the survivor has been open about her assault on campus. However, she adds that the friend told is off campus as a way of signaling that she has taken care not to break the trust of the survivor.

Perceived threat or harm constitutes the only situation that warrants breaking the survivor's confidentiality with persons on campus. The well-being of others, the survivor, and/or members of the peer network trumps confidentiality. To protect them, Bre, a junior, told others in the social circle about an assault within the group, but only after consulting the survivor first:

> The assault happened to a close friend by another friend in our friend group. The assaulter had been acting strangely since the event and was manipulating people to turn against the survivor. Once I found out the truth, I asked my close friend if I could share this information to protect our other friends from being manipulated. My close friend agreed, so I shared the information. It turns out the assaulter had been trying to do a similar thing to one of our friends, so it was a good idea. I never reached out to Title IX or anyone else, because the survivor did not want this documented in that way, however I encouraged them to, and would have supported them if they had. The assaulter ended up transferring, so my close friend dropped it because they didn't want to have to relive the experience over and over. It was not their first time they were assaulted, and they had just gotten over their past traumas.

Bre's account illustrates how the peer network can be used to socially injure survivors, as well as how the behaviors of perpetrators are often part of a pattern. Bre was aware of how the perpetrator was manipulating others within her social circle, and it was this behavior that prompted her to tell others. Bre is careful to explain that she did not take other actions, such as reporting the incident to Title IX, because the survivor did not want the incident documented. Trust has an action component, and acting according to expectation is part of what builds and sustains trustworthiness.

Conclusion

Tellings are an essential component of relational knowledge, and individuals encountering an upheaval or trauma in one's life turn to others for support and to make sense of and process what happened. This turning to rather than away from others happens even when there are substantial personal and social risks. Survivors can articulate why they tell others and how telling alleviates some of the emotional burden and makes the incident "real." They trust their friends to listen and to support them. When a telling goes poorly, survivors are also able to name how others failed to meet their expectations.

Friends, however, offer more than support; they play a major role as co-constructors of knowledge by helping survivors process what has occurred, by validating their experience, and, in some instances, by offering a narrative account of what occurred. In this collaborative role, friends are active creators and contributors to knowledge about campus sexual assault. Not enough attention focuses on the receivers of knowledge and their role as coproducers of sexual assault knowledge. While scholarly work often addresses the wrongs incurred in one's capacity as a knower (Fricker 2007), Grasswick (2018) emphasizes the need to attend to the wrongs experienced as receivers of knowledge, which occur when one is unable to trust authorities or experts for having failed to fulfill the conditions of trust (Barker et al. 2018).

Relational knowledge depends on trust for it to take hold, stick, and transform. The students who receive tellings about sexual assault are aware of the trust placed in them and, with few exceptions, treat the acquisition of this knowledge with great care even while, at times, straining under the weight of it. As a result of this hidden emotional work, friends often carry the community burden of assault, often alone (see Hirsch and Khan 2020). In academic communities, they are the muted bystanders of campus sexual assault. When they do reach out to others, they do so in ways that protect the secret and honor the trust bestowed on them.

5

Say Nothing

The Silence Holders

> I could never write out that word or give
> it sound with my tongue
> For fear that empowering it with sound
> would be admitting the tremendous
> power it had over me.
> —*Hear My Voice*

When an assault occurs, the survivor holds an experiential complexity that may or may not yet be describable via propositions, chronology, depiction, or narrative. What exactly happened and how it happened may or may not yet be understood. How one "knows" what happened may or may not be in harmony with how one's body knows. In popular culture and conventional thinking, there is a tendency to think of embodied knowing as being irrational and *less than* real knowing, but the body brings its own logic and wisdom to a situation: what is needed, what is to be avoided, when one must tread carefully, when to fight, freeze, or flee.[1] Narratives about an incident (that "something happened") and about "what happened" might arise and evolve slowly through iterations with ever more layers of complexity and insight, and over time the embodied knowledge and the storytelling-understanding might converge and entwine. Similarly, they might, over time and within and across relationships, develop because of, and converge with, the stories and understandings shared by others within a social network or community.

In the opening epigraph, a narrative begins to form from a student who had previously remained silent. Her narrative describes her hesitation and fear to name the experience and to acknowledge its effects. One senses her trepidation: if she doesn't talk about it or name it then maybe she can go on with her college experience, move on, so to speak, without any fuss, unwanted attention, or fractured friendships. Until one processes and labels an experience as an assault, one can avoid self-labeling as a victim or survivor, as well as avoid the messiness of accusation and social/relational rupture. No action is required, except, of course, the work involved in keeping it buried deep within. One senses, though, from this student's words that the incident, though unnamed and hidden, still tugs at her sense of self, its power stealth-like beneath the surface. In this way silence holding is work a survivor performs to keep from crossing a threshold irrevocable and fraught: becoming known to themselves and others as a victim, a survivor. Miller (2020, 9) explains how she stopped "when I saw the words **Rape Victim** in bold at the top of one sheet. If I refused to sign, could I remain my regular self?" But that regular self is gone for good once someone is assaulted. Telling is risky, and these students understand the power of words and "knowing with" others.

Nearly a quarter (23 percent) of the students who reported being assaulted since enrolling indicated they had not told anyone prior to our surveys. This group—the silence holders—comprises survivors who withheld their stories longer than most, choosing thus far not to share their experiences even with their closest friends. They are also secret keepers, but the secret they hold is one about themself, not a secret shared with others. Why? Their generosity and courage to break their silence via our anonymous surveys allowed us to explore the epistemic complexities they faced. This chapter examines their experiences, challenges, and choices, often in their own words.

The Perils of Telling

To begin, within our society's intersecting cultures and ideologies, sex talk is difficult even in the best of circumstances. The stakes become more significant when the sex talk that one engages in with another involves sexual violence. Survivors who hold a story or aspects of an emergent narrative, but refrain from telling even their closest friends, let alone the authorities, use silence as a discursive strategy that protects individuals, peer networks, and even institutions. Silence controls the flow of information about self and others. This silence, though acoustically similar to the quiet associated with introspection and tranquility, resides instead in intimidation and repression. Solnit (2017, 17–18) adds, "What is unsaid because introspection and serenity are sought is different from what is not said because the threats are high, or the barriers are as great as swimming is from drowning." Though we cannot know if these silence holders are drowning, we can say, given the choppy waters, that their swim must be exhausting.

In a rape culture, venturing into first tellings is perilous, a gamble predicated on trust in others (Lewis 2007) and the community and, to a lesser extent, confidence in local institutional processes and procedures. Rape culture is beset with belief systems that project doubt, blame, and shame on survivors and project innocence and "best intentions" on perpetrators. Survivors are familiar with the commonly used reactionary tropes of revenge, jealousy, deceitfulness, hysteria, "social climbing," or political motivations used to discredit their stories. As college-age adults, they are likewise familiar with the tropes and myths that reaffirm the entitlements to transgress that come with privilege as being "normal," meaning there is nothing to know here, such as, "Well, what did you expect? Boys will be boys." Alternatively, "He would never do something like that!" And who can forget, "But he has such a great future ahead of him!"[2] Silence resides in the shadows cast by the blinding glare of rape culture.

Telling involves stepping out into the light of rape culture. As Goffman (1983) astutely notes, once a person commits to talk, it places everyone in jeopardy (37), including institutions and the culture itself. Silence provides an illusion of stability. Survivors know that telling poses challenges and potentially damages one's selfhood, identity, and social relationships. Alcoff (2018), a feminist philosopher and survivor, describes the costs of telling as "being tarred for life with an identity that can affect how one is interpreted henceforth on all manner of issues, from feminism in general to legal issues to political orientation. We remember who tells us they were raped. Survivors have to negotiate these multiple considerations to decide whether to speak, how, where, and to whom" (42). Keeping silent about one's experience involves identity work. In these instances, the identity work is around what is not shared instead of what is shared about the self (see Mullaney 2006). It allows one to continue "to pass" as the person one was before the incident. Some of this awareness of risk and its attendant caution is certainly cognitive, calculated, and measured. Some of it, we know now, is deeply visceral. Consider, for example, the dilemma faced by a woman who has experienced something that doesn't rise to the behavioral definition of rape: she doesn't want to be the person, "that girl" known for making "a stink" about something she knows many within her friendship circle and community will perceive as "not that big a deal," as if having a right to bodily autonomy is not a big enough deal to be rightly expected, even demanded. Add other complexities—such as that she was a friend of the person who did this, perhaps they were alone at her place watching a movie. Maybe he is a person well-liked within the friendship network. Or he might be a highly regarded athlete or community leader. She might assume others in the community haven't experienced anything like this: being bodily violated by someone they trusted, let alone by him. She might assume others in the community, even if they were to believe her, might not see it as a violation at all. Does she tell them—one of her closest friends, perhaps? Or warn anyone?

We asked the silence holders to select the individual, situational, and relational factors that played a major or minor role in their decision not to tell anyone. The top four factors selected as major influences were the following:

I thought I could handle it on my own (56 percent)
The situation felt ambiguous (50 percent)
I wanted to move on with my life (44 percent)
I didn't want to talk about something so personal (39 percent)

Three of the top four reasons reference how the student wants to handle the situation: individually, expediently, and privately. The reluctance to talk about something so personal points to the power of telling rules around sex. Some things are best kept to oneself, not openly discussed with others. Foucault (2019) called attention to the modern prudishness associated with sex and the need to subjugate sex even at the level of language—hence the need to expunge it from things that are said. Survivor speech is excluded speech, regulated by a myriad of rules that are often more implicit than explicit (Alcoff and Gray 1993).

Survivors' reasons for keeping silent reflect internal deliberations that keep them in the driver's seat.[3] They understand that telling others could result in their life or college experience taking an unplanned detour, so it's best to manage the incident through a display of heroic individualism. For those who think they can handle it, why would they involve others? A student who had an encounter with a faculty member illustrates this sentiment: "It was in his office. He put his hand on my shoulder and then on my thigh. I looked at the door and stood. He put his hand between my legs but I said 'No' loudly. Then he stammered an apology and I said, 'I won't tell.' I have no interest in going through that. Don't touch me again. He didn't." This student was clear that she was not about to upend her college experience by telling others about what happened. His apology was enough to safeguard her secret.

Silence, as Zerubavel (2006) points out, is about more than an absence of speech; silence requires active avoidance, and "wanting to handle it on their own" or "to move on" *demands* it. To story their experience, to pull into the foreground what they have heretofore kept in the background, was perhaps made possible by the anonymity of the survey and their imagining us, the questioners, as attentive and compassionate. Regardless of why they chose to tell us, their telling required they confront and compose a narrative regarding what they had been minimizing. We have no way of knowing how many respondents were unable to categorize their experience and check the box that identifies their experience as unwanted and nonconsensual.

What Are You Gonna Do?

Survivors have probably witnessed how *tellings* played out for friends or in social media and have likely personally experienced at one time or another the negative effects of trusting others with a story only to have others doubt them. Sonya, one of our silence holders, was raped in high school and violated again in college. To explain why she had not told anyone about the college incident, she reflects on her rape in high school and her friends' reactions when she told them:

> The summer before my senior year of high school, I was raped by two men. One was someone I was "dating" at the time, the other was a stranger who the former brought along to rape me. I was heavily drunk. I told a few friends, most of whom didn't believe me. I did not reach out to "authority," adults, my parents, etc. It took me over a year to accept that what happened was rape. Additionally, there are too many "minor" incidents to recall/count/retell here. Being a woman is facing violence daily. I am constantly discovering how my growth has been affected by / hindered by male violence.

Sonya's vulnerability and willingness to risk a telling with those close to her were met with disbelief. If those close to her rejected her account, why would she trust others, particularly those with authority, to believe her?

For Sonya and others, a telling does not always produce the intended consequences or outcomes they seek. Hurdles must be cleared, and lacunae must be bridged or circumvented to be genuinely heard and believed. Sonya appears to have learned the lesson from her earlier high school telling: best to keep some things to yourself—at least for now. She points out the quotidian nature of violence against women, so *unremarkable* that it is part of what it means to be a woman. She is aware that though society may label these experiences as minor— she puts "minor" in quotes to register her critique of this label—these encounters have affected her development.

The ubiquity of sexual violence is a common theme in student comments. Students dismiss the everyday incidents as too common to register a response, certainly too common to quantify. The only way to make sense of it all is to bracket it, mark it as minor, and integrate it into what it means to be a woman or genderqueer. Too exhausting to demand a reaction every single time, they normalize, minimize, and habituate to their environment. Chris explains it this way, "I am so numb to male violence that it is difficult for me to remember if I was harmed in those ways (or more 'serious' ways)—often incidents don't seem memorable enough for me to mark them in my mind—because they are such a common occurrence. I have been trained and groomed to absorb male violence without complaint or incident since I was born into this world and structure. (I am using 'male' because it is overwhelmingly male but I acknowledge any human regardless of gender is capable of violence an assault)." Chris has become numb to gender violence, suggesting that she has disassociated from its impact on her. Like Sonya, Chris uses quotation marks to denote societal definitions like serious and perhaps to mark these labels as contested rather than shared. When does harm become serious enough to mark it in one's mind? Chris notes that part of her socialization includes the injunction to remain quiet, not to complain, and to brush off the everyday acts of misogyny. For these students, gender violence is a "background element in their lives, a footnote on every page, a cloud in every sky" (Solnit 2017, 34).

The tendency to minimize the incident, to label it as "not that bad" if it did not involve penetrative sex, if there are no physical injuries, if one knows the person, if one can chalk it up to a misunderstanding, a misread cue, provides survivors with cognitive strategies for rebracketing the experience. Though some silence holders claim it is not a big deal to absorb male violence, the experience is not without impact. These silence holders score only slightly lower on the impact scales, more often falling in the minor to moderate categories compared to respondents who tell others. Their experiences, however much they normalize them, do have an impact. For example, several silence holders described their fear or terror during a bar or club encounter. Here are three:

> The times this has happened it's been a stranger while dancing in a club setting and won't let go or take a hint. They are very forceful and often times make you scared to leave the situation.
>
> I was at a bar in CITY with a couple of friends and some older guy came up to me and seemed nice and offered to buy us all drinks. Then he started trying to make out with me and touched my inner thigh and grabbed my groin without my consent. He then proceeded to get angry when I tried to reject and stop him. It was terrifying.
>
> We were at a party and I was waiting in line for the bathroom alone and he came up and tried to kiss me and I said no thanks and he got angry pushing me against the wall forcing his hand into my shorts.

In these instances, the respondents are in a public space where others could, hopefully, intervene on their behalf. Nevertheless, these experiences appear to be so much a part of the female experience that women write them off as "just what it means to be a woman." Jen, who at the time of the survey was also a silence holder, connects her violation by a student leader to many other incidents she has experienced: "He fondled my breasts as he helped me put on a jacket I was borrowing (as he grabbed the lapels to 'fix' the jacket's placement). I may have pushed his hands away and he smiled at me, thinking it was flirtatious behavior. Other incidents are so 'run-of-the-mill' that I remember them in small moments but they tend to run together. Being at parties (on and/off campus) and having men touch my butt, waist, hips, breasts, etc. 'casually,' 'by accident,' or as they walked by me. Additionally street harassment is an almost daily occurrence in my life." Some silences are imposed within while other silences coalesce around external pressures to ignore that which rape culture defines as "run-of-the-mill," a "joke," or an "accidental touch." Rather than being distinct, these forms of silence are mutually reinforcing, offering sustenance to others so they thrive (Solnit 2017). Danielle calls out rape culture as part of how the world works: "This kind of shit happens a lot and it's not really something I want to make a big stink about for myself because it happens and people have it much worse and what are you gonna do, that's how the world works. But that's just my opinion for me. For other people, ya'll should step up your game and try to care." Though she is unwilling to make a "big stink about it," Danielle challenges others to step up and care. Knowing with others carries responsibility.

How do these daily incidents serve as a reference to others deemed more serious, what others refer to as the "real" rapes? When it comes to sexual assault, the cultural stereotype of what constitutes a "real rape" and what constitutes a justifiable concern often forms part of the interpretive backdrop to decoding what occurred. "Real rapes," so it goes, include force and physical harm or at least threat of harm. "Real" assaults place the onus of responsibility on the survivor to communicate "No! Stop!" or to physically resist. It is not uncommon to hear survivors describe themselves as lucky—lucky to be alive, lucky to have not been seriously physically injured, lucky it was only "minor," lucky someone heard and intervened, lucky to have witnesses, and so on.

I Should Have Known Better

Imagined reactions of others that discredit, distance, or doubt operate as a sort of relational power to refuse knowing-with that is "everywhere and always alive" (Foucault 1977, 177). Instead of thinking of silence holding as the result of decision-making that weighs risks, Dotson (2011) contends that self-silencing, a form of self-editing, is a form of coercive silencing because it is the result of the anticipated reaction of others. Rather than being self-imposed, silence is the result of expected reactions, the skepticism of friends and family, and the societal expectation that one should "know better." Alexa could not offer any details of her assault because it "was too hard to talk about." She did acknowledge that others have said she was "unclear with my boundaries and I should know better to say out loud my uncomfortability." She adds, "It is just hard as a woman as it always your fault and you should know better than having guys over late at night. It should not be talked about this." Alexa acknowledges that sometimes nonverbal cues, having someone over to your place late at night, can be misread. Inviting a man over late at night could be code for sex, a "booty" call, but, of course, without direct conversation, its meaning is unclear—it could just as easily be code for "let's watch a movie." Alexa's admonishment that "she should know better" draws on her lived experience of gender dynamics, and sadly, her interpretation is supported by previous research. Men are more likely to interpret everyday actions and body language as indicative of consent (Sandoz and Louisiana Contextual Science Research Group 2021), and when they do, women too often blame themselves.

The sexual implications of getting together are difficult to discuss and clarify, either before, to clarify the meaning of the situation, or after, to clarify what happened. Naomi blames herself for not knowing better: "He was a fuckboy and I was innocent. I didn't know better but should have." For women, knowing better implies moving through the world with the understanding that you can be assaulted and that it is *your* responsibility to reduce the risks—don't invite guys over late at night, especially fuckboys. You are supposed to know who the fuckboys are, and what that means. In Naomi's case, since her perpetrator had a reputation for being a jerk and a player, she should have been more cautious. Her reference to her innocence may suggest a certain sexual inexperience and/or naivete about heteronormative sexual relations. Naomi's and Alexa's comments imply that they were supposed to have already possessed this knowledge about how to avoid sexual assault. Note that these survivors do not assign responsibility, at least in these accounts, to their perpetrators' failures of "knowing better"—for not asking if Alexa and Naomi wanted to have sex and/or for not inquiring about what they wanted to happen.

I Didn't Say "No," but I Didn't Say "Yes"

Sometimes an incident resides in a liminal space shrouded by uncertainties, confusion, and other ambiguities. The shifting definitions and understandings of what constitutes assault and the evolving gender norms related to sexual expression and desire create fertile ground for second-guessing what happened and how to understand it. The social and legal scripts for what constitute an assault are so limited that experiences that don't conform to these scripts remain hermeneutically adrift. The schema of nonconsent mirrors what people imagine constitutes a sexual assault (Featherstone et al. 2024). Our conversations with students suggest, for instance, that they struggle to understand the changing legal definitions of assault and the changing normative context for conveying consent. For instance, regarding the definition of rape, it was not until 2013 that the federal definition changed to include other orifices besides the vagina, making it possible to include male and trans individuals as rape survivors. Similarly, it is still culturally ingrained to assume the gender of sexual assault survivors must be female. You, as reader, can be forgiven, for example, if you assumed all the silence holders were women. They were not.

Recent changes in definitions of consent add to this complexity. Many colleges and universities have adopted affirmative consent standards, which stipulate that consent be communicated through words or actions in explicit, ongoing, and unambiguous ways. The adoption of affirmative consent standards by many colleges and universities changes the terms of sexual discourse. Aimed at shifting the college culture around sexual engagement, affirmative consent encourages greater sexual agency and clearer communication. Affirmative consent challenges sexual beliefs that assume one can forge ahead until one encounters resistance either verbally or physically. It is no longer about "no" and all about "yes." An absence of agreement through silence, passivity, or submission fails to convey consent (Featherstone et al. 2024).

Colleges and universities often introduce students to their consent policies as part of sexual assault prevention training, often embedded in first-year orientation. How is consent defined by this college?[4] Does it require a yes or a no? Must it be communicated verbally, and does it need to be ongoing? How does the use of alcohol and drugs affect one's ability to consent? A popular training video likens consent to asking for a cup of tea. Designed to be accessible and nonthreatening, the video attempts to normalize sexual discourse by reframing it as ordinary—as simple as asking someone if they would like tea. However, talking about sexual desire is not ordinary, certainly not akin to asking for tea. Talking about sex is laden with social complexity; social and political forces influence one's ability to speak up. Keri explains, "I think it's really hard for younger students to distinguish between characterizations of actions and situations. I noticed even in myself struggling with how drugs and alcohol, perceptions of roles, and perceptions of expectations make us less likely to believe that something is unwanted. I have found myself trying to convince myself during the act that I did want it even though I didn't, because I felt like I should." Keri identifies several factors that complicate consent: the use of drugs and alcohol, gendered expectations around sex—that is, who is perceived as the initiator and the gatekeeper, and the relationship between feelings and actions. She describes the inner dialogue that occurs between what she wants and prevailing cultural or social pressures, what she describes as the "should." Her comments support previous studies of consent among college students that reveal the conflicting tension between internal desires, external pressures and actions, and expectations (some internalized). These studies show that women are less likely to act on their *own* desires and more likely to focus on the needs of the other. Going along with others' wants and desires, even if they involve engaging in unwanted behavior, is sometimes easier than saying no (Featherstone et al. 2024).

It is in this contested discursive space that some students struggle to find the words. Some silence holders adopt a schema of consent that prioritizes verbal resistance over the positive expression of yes. Absent from their account is an expectation that their partner will check in with them periodically to see if they are comfortable and if they consent before proceeding. Rather, they talk about their responsibility to stop it, to say "No!" Brianna says, "I wasn't forced to perform oral sex without my consent, but I know that I didn't want to do it either, but because I didn't speak up or share those feelings I can't say if it happened without my consent." Brianna doesn't mention if her partner asked her if she wanted to engage in oral sex. Her comments draw on sexual scripts that place the burden of responsibility on the survivor to stop unwanted sexual activity, not on the perpetrator to ask for consent. Brianna is clear that something unsettling and undesired happened, but she is unclear whether what happened was consensual. Brianna's experience is wedged between competing notions of consent: one that requires that she resist verbally and one that asks her to express her sexual agency. The yes means yes approach of affirmative consent falters in a culture in which sex talk falls outside permissible speech for women and those who are genderqueer (Featherstone et al. 2024).

Speaking up about sex is difficult, and for some, talking about sexual wants and desires is dicey. In a culture in which women and genderqueer persons can be labeled or sanctioned for expressing their sexuality, there isn't much space to talk about or even discover what one wants. Sometimes one may discover, in the moment, that one isn't comfortable with a particular practice. Orenstein (2024) describes an increasingly common practice among young adults of choking their partner during sex. She cites research that shows that nearly two-thirds of women in a campus-representative survey of five thousand students at an anonymized midwestern university said a partner had choked them during sex. Among younger girls, aged twelve to seventeen, the incidence of sexual strangulation had increased to 40 percent. Survey respondents indicated that their partners never or only sometimes asked before choking, and many say that there were moments in which they couldn't breathe or speak, affecting their ability to give consent. In a different study by the same researchers, choking was among the most frequently listed sex acts young women said scared them, reporting that it sometimes made them worry whether they'd survive. Though many of the girls and women with whom Orenstein spoke didn't want or enjoy being choked, they didn't identify it as assault.

Apart from whether hesitation would be noticed and whether a "no" would be heard and respected, it can sometimes be difficult to know if you desire or enjoy a particular experience until you experience it. In a few instances, students described consenting to a set of sexual practices only to find themselves experiencing something to which they hadn't offered their consent. A student who consented to engage in protected sex later found the other person engaging "in intercourse with me without wearing a condom or asking for consent." Amaya, another silence holder who had been interested in a "hookup," was thrown off "by the oral anal play without asking. I froze and didn't know how to handle it because I had been drinking and I had led him on." They may feel embarrassed by their naivete or lack of sexual experience or confused because though they did desire some sexual engagement, what they thought they consented to turns into something quite different.

Uncertainty is exacerbated when alcohol and drugs are present. Though students express less ambiguity about an experience if someone has blacked out, in cases in which they are buzzed or under the influence, their inability to recall what happened with clarity leads to greater self-blame and/or a reason to dismiss the behavior of the perpetrator. Sophie was silent about her experience because she was unsure if her partner was aware that she was unable to give consent: "Consent had been given before and it may not have been apparent to the other person that I was not entirely 'there' and able to give consent. It's difficult for me to judge how aware or not they were of the situation." Dylan describes an encounter in which he had been drinking with friends. The next morning, he could recall very little of what had happened the previous evening: "I came back from a night of drinking at the club with a bunch of friends. I was heading back to my room with one girl that I was hooking up with prior and woke up in my room with someone else. I have memory of perhaps two seconds of this encounter. It felt weird because I wouldn't say that I was entirely opposed to hooking up with this girl while sober. However, I still didn't feel too good about the actions of that night." Dylan doesn't feel good about what happened, and although he doesn't name what occurred, he has identified his experience as nonconsensual, unwanted sex.

When Friends Are Involved

Silence is more than an individual decision; it has social properties that reflect the imagined reactions of and impact on others. It's much harder to reduce the sexual encounter to a simple binary of yes or no when there are relationships at play: boyfriends, friends, even family (Featherstone et al. 2024). In addition to protecting oneself against harmful scrutiny, silence can also be used to protect others. For silence holders who selected "wanted to move on" as a major reason for not telling, they were much more likely also to select the major reason being that the assault involved a friend.

When the assault involves someone in one's network, telling threatens one's social capital and friendships. Relational considerations are strong motivations to keep silent. Much of the literature on disclosures focuses on the effects of information sharing on the self. Our research highlights how information strategies are just as much about relational networks as they are about self. As Elena explains, "It's not really a nice thing to think about that your friends might have sexually assaulted you." Assaults violate taken-for-granted assumptions that a friend will not harm you, will respect your boundaries, will listen to you, and will be attentive to your verbal and nonverbal cues, which are parts of what it means to be a friend. Silence holders struggle to reconcile those contradictory experiences.

When the perpetrator is a close friend or ex-partner, telling, even within one's intimate circle, threatens to strain or dissolve relational ties. The relational fallout goes beyond the specific connection to the perpetrator; it extends into the network. Khan et al.'s (2018) findings make clear that a telling is much more than a simple dyadic exchange; it is an intervention into network bonds. Marissa's first-time telling unpacks this larger relational context:

> An ex-boyfriend who was still a good friend of mine and I were hanging out and drinking alcohol. We began to kiss and touch each other and we had just began to have sex. I sometimes suffer from panic attacks during sex and I felt a lot of anxiety suddenly and felt a panic attack coming on. So, I audibly asked him to stop. He ignored me. I asked him to get off of me, to let me go to stop, etc. And, he just ignored me and continued to force himself inside of me. I began to cry and physically hit him. He was on top of me and held my arms. He was substantially stronger than me and continued until he finished. I did cry and yell but when it was over I didn't leave. I was too drunk to drive and didn't fully understand what had happened. He was an undocumented person and I also knew him and his family quite well. Having told someone would result in his deportation along with his daughter's sister's and other family members who were also living undocumented. His entire family also depended solely on his income. Hurting them so much, especially his mother whose health was so bad that her life depended on medication paid for by his money, would not have brought me any justice. It would have brought further injustice to other innocent people. That is why I decided not to tell anyone.

Marissa takes great care to include details, such as saying "no" and fighting back, that define, at least in legal terms, that she was raped. Even with those details, she admits that she was unsure how to define what happened, most probably because of their relational ties and history. Her account brings into sharp focus the relational web that influences her decision to not tell and how telling pits one form of injustice against another one.

Positive emotions, such as feeling attraction or "liking" the other person, add to the internal conflict and confusion. When there is "mutual attraction" it is harder for the survivor to describe the experience as nonconsensual. Theresa says, "We were kind of seeing each other, and I didn't know if I wanted it to happen or not but felt pressured, because I really liked him." Feelings cloud the definition of the incident. Hye suggests that her perpetrator took advantage of her feelings: "I'm not really sure if it was sexual assault or not, but I was touched nonconsensually by a friend. He took advantage of me because he knew I had feelings for him so he figured he could touch me, but I didn't reciprocate because he had a girlfriend." These silence holders were much more likely to shroud the incident in ambiguity, miscommunication even, to preserve their perception of the friend: "There was miscommunication about the terms of our friendship. Things were uncomfortable for a while, but we remained friends."

Rather than making a scene and causing a major disruption in the social circle, these silence holders opt to handle it by assigning it to a liminal space between a yes or a no, or by responding indirectly. Shandra, who was an underclassman, describes how alcohol provided an excuse for her social circle to dismiss what was happening as mere hijinks:

> A friend/acquaintance had had too much to drink at a party, and kept trying to dance with me when I made it clear I did not want to dance with them. They kept stumbling and falling onto my lap and privates, grabbing and trying to fondle me and play it off as an accident. All of their friends thought it was funny but it was just super annoying and I was tempted to punch them in the face after the third or fourth time, but the individual and all their friends were upperclassmen so I felt pressured to stay at the party. Eventually they did this one too many times and tried to slide their hand down my pants as I was helping them up and I walked out of the party.

Shandra describes the social pressure to play along with the situation, restraining the impulse to punch the person, and instead opting to leave instead of making a scene. Clearly, the decision to leave the party instead of hitting the other student, a so-called friend, was aimed at preserving the social relations of the peer group, albeit a group actively belittling her experience and jeopardizing her social belonging.

Far from the affirmative consent framework in which consent is secured before advances are made, these silence holders offer descriptions in which they feel responsible for fending off sexual advances. Serena, who was off campus attending an art event with friends, elaborates,

> We stayed at one of the friends' boyfriends' house for the night. The boyfriend had a friend that also stayed at the house that night. The sleeping arrangements were my friend and her boyfriend in one bed and my other friend and I in the pullout bed in one of the couches and the boyfriend's friend was going to sleep on one of the other couches. However, it was incredibly cold that night and the house did not have heat. So my friend suggested that the boyfriend's friend come join us so we could all stay warm. When he came to join us my friend immediately fell asleep and I was in the middle. I was trying to fall asleep however, he kept trying to put his hand down my pants and was groping me. I kept pushing his hands away and pretending to be asleep. Eventually he stopped and I fell asleep.

Serena describes a situation in which the boyfriend's friend takes advantage of circumstances to initiate sexual contact without consent. He does not ask her before he initiates touch. She responds to his advances by pushing his hand away, an unambiguous action that clearly communicates her nonconsent. Like with other narratives, to convey her nonconsent this woman relied on non-verbal cues, which were ignored. Research shows that women will often rely on nonverbal actions, the pushing away of the hand, the decision to change seats or leave a party, to convey their nonconsent. However, if the other party fails to respect these cues, survivors often blame themselves for not saying no. They question whether *they* were clear enough. Khan et al. (2018) found in their interviews with survivors that keeping an experience ambiguous allows for social continuity rather than social rupture, and this form of "productive ambiguity" guards one's identity, networks, and plans.

Silent Partners in the Whisper Network

Silences in the dominant discursive community rarely translate into total silence. People often find ways to share information even if it is limited, as Zerubavel (2006) explains, to conversations that happen in the nooks and crannies of discourse or, in our case, in comments shared on a climate survey. Medina (2013) describes how the gay community had ways of sharing information about places and people to avoid and ways to stay safe long before these issues were part of the dominant discourse. Whisper networks abound. Certainly, within our campus community, students are whispering and, when necessary, signaling without speaking—the unspeakable things not quite spoken, pointing to the unremarkable. Contrary to our initial speculations that this group might be isolated, we discovered that most silence holders had friends or peers confide in them about their assault. Perhaps their friends knew they could be trusted, part of tacit knowledge or an unspoken vibe that can be communicated without words. The children of Holocaust survivors knew about their parents' trauma even though their parents did not speak about their past (Kidron 2009). The need for safety and knowledge sharing creates communicative pathways, nods and whispered warnings, even if persons are unable to share their stories within the dominant discursive space (Alcoff 2018, 38). The things one does not say or is prohibited from saying, Foucault (2019) maintains, exist alongside the things said.

One might think that a friend's telling would provide a context for disclosing a shared experience. Gabby admits that she thinks her friend "shared hoping I would tell them what happened to me." Perhaps the silence holders who are part of the whisper network understand that being a good listener demands they be fully present to the teller—it's not the time to redirect the conversation back to them. We don't know because we didn't ask this question. What we do know is that the silence holders who are part of the whisper network are similar to and different from the secret keepers. They, too, indicate that they listened closely to what their friend shared with them and that they believed them. All the silence holders in the whisper network rejected the statement that the person confiding in them had misunderstood the situation or was exaggerating. In short, silence holders are believers. So, how are silence holders different from those survivors who have shared their experience with others?

Silence holders were less likely than secret keepers to follow up with any action after being told. They were less likely than the secret keepers to encourage their fellow survivors to talk about it, to anyone. Only 15 percent of silence holders encouraged their friends to seek support from college resources, compared to 33 percent of secret keepers. Moreover, they were less likely to check in on their fellow survivor following the telling than secret keepers (23 vs. 62 percent, $p < .01$) and less likely to tell them it wasn't their fault (31 vs. 70 percent, $p < .01$). Compared to secret keepers who expressed a desire to engage in campus activism around sexual assault (30 percent), a smaller percentage of silence holders (8 percent) indicated they wanted to do more on campus to prevent sexual assault. Due to the small number of silence holders, we interpret these findings with some caution. We did find a similar pattern in the AAU climate data. Those who didn't tell and suspected a friend had been assaulted were more likely to indicate that they "did nothing" compared to those survivors who told others.

Silence holders turn in and away from their experience rather than turning toward others. Their "knowing of" others does not translate into "knowing with" others. In their cases, personal knowledge does not get transformed into social knowledge, and hence personal knowledge fails to reposition the issue from an individual one to a social one.

Conclusion: Silence as Strategy

Silence holders choose silence as an informational and relational strategy. Their silence is not based on a naive understanding of the world, nor on a lack of knowledge about institutional policies and services. Rather, it is based upon a realistic, informed assessment—an acquired "knowing better" that leads them to ask astutely, "What good would come of telling?" Silence holders seek to escape the stigma and far-reaching negative consequences that rape culture assigns to those assaulted. Their silence controls the damaging information that others would use to discredit their experience. By keeping silent, the survivor conceals information that others could use to impugn their character or to question their decision-making.

In addition, silence holding preserves relational webs of affiliation; it doesn't require the person to cut off or thwart the possibility of moving into new relational circles. It sidesteps the relational friction when friends within a network feel like they must pick sides and/or the complicated affective terrain, the relational betrayal, associated with attributing malevolence to a friend. Silence allows the survivor to remain in control of the very definition of the situation—making room for minimization (it's not a big deal), normalization (it happens to lots of women or trans individuals), and plausible deniability (it wasn't really assault or rape). One doesn't risk having one's story and integrity challenged by another's viewpoint. Silence holders endeavor "to pass" as the person they were before the assault, which reflects their deep desire to hold onto their lives and their sense of belonging and direction, including retaining the academic and social goals and dreams they held before the assault. Remaining in control of one's story, even if that story includes an important omission, serves important social and identity-building functions that include "holding fast to a friend group or extracurricular activity or securing an identity as a cool girl, competent partier, or successful socializer" (Khan et al. 2018, 452). Coming to terms with what has happened is a social process that has implications for identities, relationships, and imagined futures. Not telling "allows them to psychologically downplay the experience, to avoid confronting it regularly, to refuse to see themselves as victims, to persuade themselves that a very difficult thing did not happen, or to continue to understand the person who assaulted them (often someone they know well and about whom they care) is a good person, friend, or partner" (436). Of course, from this perspective, silence preserves time and energy because "What are you gonna do?" But alas, holding silence is work. We know it to be, as the opening epigraph attests.

It is important to view all students, including these, as dynamic; it is not as if they are tethered permanently to any one experiential or decision-making category. Just because they were silent at the time of our survey does not mean they do not share the same understandings and deep truths (DeLaet and Mills 2018) as students who have told others. After all, by way of our anonymous survey, silence holders chose to tell *us*; that's how we learned of them.

Is silence holding equivalent to "not seeing" the elephant in the quad? Does it share a kinship with avoidance? As we have mentioned, silence holders and avoiders share a kind of reciprocity: the one dares not tell, and the other dares not hear. Some avoiders seem determined to not know, and some silence holders seem determined to minimize, tucking their experience into the background of life. The difference is the burden of holding alone the experience of something so vile. Many silence holders can acknowledge anonymously that they were bumped, perhaps hurt, perhaps worse, by an encounter with an elephant in the quad. They endeavor to proceed in a manner that does not call attention to their wounds, to proceed with their lives as if nothing happened. They have changed and remain alert. It's the cost of living. The avoiders have not yet borne that cost and haven't noticed the elephant.

Clearly, rape culture's discursive realms rely on silences and secrets to maintain speech as a locus of power and to keep others from speaking directly and loudly about sexual violence. But who is to say when silence holders might find themselves gathered with friends for dinner, and one story leads to another amid the company of attentive erstwhile avoiders, who hadn't known, who had no idea, that the epistemic possibility of knowing-with appears.

The buzz of the whisper network is heard only by students and perhaps a few trusted faculty and staff. Though silence holders are somewhat atypical in their silence within the whisper network, they, like the secret keepers, are largely silent in other parts of the epistemological field. The knowledge that moves through the whisper network does not circulate freely into other epistemic circles, particularly those that involve college authorities. The "telling-to" that exists within the whisper network is very different from the "telling-on" associated with the circulation of knowledge along more formal institutional routes.

6

Telling on Others

Sharing One's Experiences
with Title IX

In previous chapters, we focused on the *lateral* unevenness of student awareness of sexual violence within their community and what it means for them to
know or not know with survivors. In this chapter, we examine what the college seems to know officially, and how it avoids knowing more fully. While
there are myriad ways by which college officials might be notified or otherwise
learn of sexual violence incidents within the student community, here we focus
on reports and complaints arising through Title IX.[1] Tellings routed to and
through Title IX serve as the primary source of an institution's official knowledge, the term used to refer to activating knowledge that moves into formal
administrative spaces. Colleges and universities are obligated to respond to only
this form of knowledge.[2] But what form of knowledge is it really, and how much
of it arrives? And does the trickle of information that does get through this
way ever get compiled and shared with the community meaningfully, in ways
that allow the community to know more fully?

Like the tellings that circulate laterally within student networks, the tellings that move up through the institutional hierarchy are also governed by a
set of telling rules that impact how information moves into formal spaces, specifically to those spaces associated with Title IX and college administration.
When sharing their experiences with campus officials, students encounter a
mandated structure of "telling-on" rules that often override and contradict the

"telling-to" rules that operate in student whisper networks. *Telling on* someone to an authority and *telling to* a friend are separate social and interpersonal processes (Klein 2018) with distinct norms and knowledge repositories. Some telling-on rules are socially enculturated. Policy and law inscribe many Title IX telling-on rules.

Telling-On

Telling-on implies a social hierarchy with authority to deal with infractions so that one can appeal to the higher authority for remedy. The supposed authority could be a parent, for example, but it might also be the police, one's RA, coach, or team captain, or the college's Title IX officer. It could also be one's peers, at least in principle: one might think of the peer group as having some diffuse, collective authority over its members, so that one might say, for example, at one's dorm meeting, "Pat, I can't sleep with your late-night music blasting. Can we all agree to have quiet hours after one o'clock?"

Early socialization conveys important lessons about how and when to tell on a peer. Learning to keep secrets, for example, is part of that curriculum. Children as young as six years old can distinguish between secret and nonsecret matters and can offer reasons for keeping certain things secret (Misch et al. 2016). Secrets told can find their way to disapproving peers and higher authorities; in that way, divulging a secret relinquishes control. Similarly, children learn to keep some rule violations within the group—one doesn't need to be a tattletale about every rule violation. Teachers and parents encourage children to resolve some infractions within the group and, in some instances, to look the other way, as illustrated by the adage "don't be a tattletale." Being a tattletale doesn't have a positive connotation. As Corbin (2021) points out, there are not many positive words in the English language for those who tell on others. Negatives abound: snitch, tattletale, squealer, and snake in the grass, to name a few. Telling on someone's bad behavior is often considered a betrayal of the person being told on, as well as one's group. Do not get your teammate in trouble, for example.[3]

The familiar saying "no one likes a tattletale" reinforces the social repercussions of telling-on. Telling on someone, either to the group itself or to a higher authority, threatens bonds of social connection within the group. Previous research on cheating and bullying shows that young adults rarely rely on their peers for help. Even when adolescents witness cheating, they seldom call it out or report it to authorities (Waltzer et al. 2024). Their fear of social ramifications, of making enemies or being disliked, keeps them from telling on their peers even as they weigh concerns for others' welfare in their decision-making. Other studies on bullying report similar findings: young people cannot rely on the group to intercede and are reluctant to tell adults because they are concerned about escalation, about not wanting to be labeled a snitch, and not wishing to worry their parents (Lui et al. 2022). In short, telling-on is a very different social process than the telling-to that operates within relationships.

Telling Title IX

As knowledge of a sexual assault moves out of the whisper network into formal administrative spaces, an epistemic conversion changes the relational parameters from close ties to impartial ones. It changes the operative norms applicable to the telling. What was previously a telling-to becomes a telling-on. Telling-to involves friends and relies on relational norms anchored in mutuality and trust. In contrast, to deliberately tell on someone, to report an assault, presupposes the teller is at least somewhat clear that a rule has been violated and is clear that they want the authority to agree and to intervene. This is risky. To tell on someone, particularly if it is someone you know in the community, threatens norms of loyalty and catapults the teller into a bureaucratic process with its own telling rules and understandings of what it means for listeners to be trustworthy. The official Title IX telling-on process is inherently propositional and evidentiary, and the accusation is to be evaluated impartially, even skeptically, at each step in the adjudicative process. It is akin to a mechanism that once activated by the initial telling-on is designed to move toward any number of prescribed end states based upon a decision tree. The teller must trust not just the official listeners but the trustworthiness of the process itself, which is located within its adherence to its decision-making rules and preestablished end state possibilities. Derailment of the logical process is grounds for appeal, and that process, too, is similarly mechanistic. Even before telling on a peer to a Title IX officer, the complainant faces all the social stigmas and prohibitions mentioned above, such as loss of control and peer-group betrayal, not to mention any faults the process may evince. But Title IX procedures impose more prohibitions by delineating with exactitude to whom, when, and how one must tell, in the face of skepticism, including cross-examination, across multiple settings, sans mutuality. Moreover, the teller is expected to trust this adversarial process—to place their trust in the process rather than in a relationship.[4]

Telling Title IX is seldom the first telling: telling-on, officially, is typically preceded by telling friends and/or family, where virtuous listening and supportive give-and-take are more likely practiced. This prior relational telling/listening exercise might be key to survivors' decisions to seek help from Title IX, to let the college know what needs to be known so that appropriate actions can be taken. The problem is that whatever clarity and trust in their story survivors may have gained by telling friends is put up for contestation—that is, officially challenged by the telling-on procedures. The rules shift profoundly.

That survivors and their confidants confront this contested space as a wall and are hurt by it becomes another discursive feature within the whisper network. Indeed, most students who have a sexual assault experience opt to forgo telling Title IX authorities about their experiences. Their reasons, as we shall explore, have less to do with their understanding of the Title IX process and more to do with the social fallout of telling on a peer and their perceptions of the institution's trustworthiness. Negative experiences with Title IX, past and present, circulating within the whisper network shape perceptions of whether the college or university can be trusted to act on their behalf and in the community's best interests.

Minding *This* Gap: What Colleges Dare Not Know

To get a sense of the magnitude and significance of the vertical gap between the knowledge that circulates within the student whisper networks and the knowledge that college administrators possess, we need compare only those assaulted with those who report assaults. Only a small fraction of the tellings associated with sexual assault and sexual violence incidents move into formal administrative spaces through policy-driven channels. In the extensive climate survey of the Association of American Universities (2017), only 13 percent of students assaulted talked to *anyone in a university program*. Our climate surveys show similar findings. The percentage of students who shared their experience with Title IX ranges from a low of 10 percent in 2016 to a high of 17 percent in 2020. In 2022, 15 percent of students who were assaulted told someone in the Title IX office. Telling someone in the campus security office was even lower, ranging from 1 to 10 percent. A somewhat larger percentage of students tell a mental health or religious professional after some time has passed, but due to confidentiality protocols, those tellings do not pass into official channels.

Given these patterns, it is not surprising that the official knowledge reported in the annual federal Clery report shows that most colleges and universities had NO REPORTED RAPES on or off campus in 2018 through 2022. Table 1 shows the percentage of colleges and universities reporting *no* rapes on and off campus, by year, between 2018 and 2022.

The very reporting requirement intended to provide an empirical account of sexual violence on college campuses obfuscates its extent because it considers only one part of the epistemic field: the minimal, propositional knowledge that makes its way, officially, to college officials. As a result, the knowledge of sexual assault circulating to college authorities is grossly incomplete, a distortion of campus sexual assault, akin to describing Van Gogh's *Starry Night* relying only on the left corner—one misses the stars completely. Consequently, college administrators are unaware of over 80 percent of the assaults occurring

Table 1
Percentage of colleges and universities reporting no rapes

Year	On-campus rapes (% reporting 0)	Off-campus rapes (% reporting 0)
2018	87.3	91.6
2019	87.6	92.7
2020	90.3	94.8
2021	88.9	93.3
2022	88.7	92.9

SOURCE: U.S. Department of Education's Campus Safety and Security (CSS) Data Analysis Cutting Tool: https://ope.ed.gov/campussafety/# /datafile/list.

on campuses, not to mention their storied nature and the relational knowledge and experiences held by bystanders—their friends, peers, and confidants.

The Obama administration can be credited for recognizing the vertical gap and for attempting to find ways to bridge it (White House Task Force to Protect Students from Sexual Assault 2014). Noting that "schools have to get credit for being honest and for finding out what's really happening on campus" (8), the Obama White House conceded that "reports to authorities, as we know, don't really provide a fair measure of the problem" (8). The admission that reports to authorities might not be a fair measure of the problem was a bold statement with significant epistemological implications. The recognition that colleges and universities might need to get credit for finding out what was actually happening on campus suggests that institutional awareness comes with some costs or liabilities, implying that institutional interests and student interests are at odds.

The White House report (2014) urged colleges to administer campus climate surveys to fill the gap between reports and "what actually happens" on campus. When done right, campus climate surveys "can gauge the prevalence of sexual assault on campus, test students' attitudes and awareness about the issue, and provide schools with an invaluable tool for crafting solutions" (8). The right tools could increase institutional awareness and both impel and point to possible actions.

Given the conflict of interest or reluctance to assign responsibility to colleges, it was tempting and too easy for college authorities and policymakers to interpret the gap, should they acknowledge it at all, as a product of students' passive avoidance—essentially a lack of knowledge about Title IX rather than students' underlying "complicated emotions, interests, and strategic responses to injustice" (DeLaet and Mills 2018, 502). By this thinking, the gap existed because students did not know how to report their assaults or feared their reports would not be handled confidentially and adjudicated fairly. Campus climate surveys could fill the gap by monitoring the extent of sexual violence on campuses and students' understanding of Title IX processes—or so the narrative goes. Educational campaigns about Title IX have increased on campuses; student onboarding often includes Title IX training. To some extent, these training courses have increased knowledge about Title IX. More students report that they know about the Title IX process. Of the thousands of students in the AAU climate survey, 56 percent of students indicated they were somewhat to extremely knowledgeable about how to report sexual misconduct to the university. Over three-fourths of students at our institution indicate they have received training in the college policies and procedures.

Despite an increase in overall knowledge about Title IX, students are less familiar with the technical language of the Title IX process; that is, survivors are complainants, and alleged perpetrators are respondents. Students who talk with Title IX officials "make a report," but reports are not "formal complaints" (which require investigations), and sanctions are issued only in response to a complaint. Fewer students, just over half of those responding to our survey, reported that they understood the difference between reporting an incident to Title IX and filing a formal complaint. Only 36 percent of the students responding to the AAU climate surveys indicate they are somewhat to extremely knowledgeable about what happens when one reports sexual misconduct to the university. Campus climate surveys measure gains in student knowledge about reporting and identify areas that need further clarification.

Though some elements of the reporting process confuse students, students are clear about the reasons they do not report their assaults to an institutional authority. Their reasons have little to do with a lack of knowledge about the Title IX process. For example, a lack of knowledge about the reporting process or "to whom or where to go" does not appear among the most frequently cited reasons for not reporting.

In the AAU climate survey, over half of survivors of forced and incapacitated rape or sexual battery indicated that they did not report the incident because they "didn't think it was serious enough." Our survey finds similar patterns. When asked why they did not report, students frequently cite they didn't think it was that "big a deal." The normalization of gender violence is so internalized that rape is not severe enough to warrant action, particularly if there are no cuts, bruises, or broken bones—and there are those as well!—even though the assault was serious enough for the student to experience a range of physical, emotional, behavioral, and psychological impacts. Other reasons for not reporting to Title IX include embarrassment or shame, a perception that "nothing will be done," fear of the social consequences, and a reluctance to get the perpetrator in trouble.

Students describe situations involving friends, ex-partners, or members of their social networks. They understand the social costs of telling on someone they know. Tess describes a situation that involves a close friend with whom she had a previous sexual encounter. She had communicated that she did not want to continue a sexual relationship with him. When he started touching her at a party, she says, "I felt trapped socially because none of my friends realized what was going on and I felt that if I made a fuss about it, it would make a scene and that scared me." She no longer interacts with this person but has not told anyone else because she does not want to affect how her other friends interact with him. These survivors sought other ways to handle the situation, such as cutting off contact or talking through what happened with the other person, in some instances. Hana, who describes an experience with a person she had previously hooked up with, had tried to stop the sexual encounter by saying, "I am not comfortable hooking up with a drunk person," which didn't stop her from touching her. She acknowledges that despite the experience, they are still friends. As one student explains, "Telling people would lead to harmful effects on others' lives."

For some survivors, fear of their perpetrator keeps them from telling administrators (or anyone). Kamala shares that he told her, "Shut up before I make you shut up." Daniele describes a violent encounter because of her failure to wake up her assailant for a popular dining hall meal:

> He woke up and started screaming at me. He pulled my hair and grabbed my arms and threw me to the ground. He told me not to make any noise or else he'd make sure I wouldn't speak again. He was 215 pounds and I am 135 pounds. He was 6'2" and I am 5'7". I was terrified. I woke up the next morning with bruises all over me and had to wear big baggy clothes the next day. I was in so much pain all day. I was in fear if anyone saw anything I would get in more trouble with him so I took a lot of Advil and pretended everything was fine.

Telling-on does carry risks, and some students understand how going to an authority puts them at risk for greater harm. Like Daniele's, Tasha's perpetrator threatened to hurt her and used a variety of controlling tactics to ensure her silence.

> He threatened to hurt me and tried to make me come back to his dorm when I tried to break up with him after I found out he cheated on me with five other women and guilted me about it by inclining that he had to do that because I wasn't a good partner. He only gave me attention and made me feel wanted when I wanted to leave. He told friends he wanted to beat me up or physically hurt me with purposeful intent when I was being "annoying." He would sometimes grab me in a harmful way or try to force me to do things by pinning

me down and not listening to me. Would raise his voice at me to scare me,
knew that raising his voice and walking towards me scared me due to past
trauma. Tried to propose to me to keep me in the relationship. This happened
over a span of three months.

These reasons, some about personal safety, some more social and relational, still
others linked to perceived institutional efficacy, contribute to students not telling the college—a selective silence, as most do tell their friends. Doubling
down on Title IX education may serve institutional interests, but it does nothing to address the factors these students identify as important in their
decision-making.

Telling on an on-campus peer presents survivors with a steep relational wall
to scale.[5] Once cleared, the student encounters a new set of telling rules that
operate within a contradictory space of competing claims. To be heard, their
experience and account must conform to these telling codes (Alcoff and Gray
1993), and unlike the whisper network, this administrative process is designed
to be neutral.

The Telling-On Rules and Procedures

Formal telling rules about sexual violence are embedded, most often, in mandated Title IX policies and processes. These rules direct students to the appropriate people to tell (the who) and to the process (the how). Many colleges and
universities outline these steps on their website. One purpose of formalizing
the telling rules in this way is to increase institutional knowledge of and responsiveness to sexual assaults while still protecting individual survivors' privacy,
admirable goals, certainly. The epistemic reach of the process is severely limited,
not least of all because it is geared to receive and test truth-verifiable propositions, or to know-that. Choosing to know about sexual assault this way and
only this way, transactionally, is choosing to not know the important thing. It
is a version of avoidance. "Knowing with survivors" is displaced, if not repudi-
ated, by this procedure, which, not surprisingly, displaces the knowing most
likely to activate a moral imperative to intervene.

Whom to Tell

Formal telling rules stress the importance of talking to persons in official roles
shrouded in confidentiality so that survivors can make decisions at their own
pace without worrying about what their peers might think about their decision to report an assault. The Obama administration's communications protocol notes that some survivors "don't want their assailants or the assailant's
friends, classmates, teammates, or club members to know they've reported what
happened. But they do want someone on campus to talk to—and many want

to talk in confidence, so they can sort through their options at their own pace. If victims don't have a confidential place to go or think a school will launch a full-scale investigation against their wishes, many will stay silent" (White House Task Force to Protect Students from Sexual Assault 2014, 11). Students do want to talk, and they are reluctant to tell on peers. However, as we have shown, they do not stay silent. Rather than avoiding their peers, they often rely on members of their friendship networks to sort through their options first.

The White House protocol identified three groups with whom a survivor could talk: (1) those college employees required to maintain near confidentiality, such as pastoral or mental health counselors;[6] (2) other employees who are required to report an incident to the college without any identifying information; and (3) responsible employees, or mandatory reporters, who are required to report information about an assault to the Title IX coordinator. All three groups must abide by institutional or professional telling rules that require them to keep the telling confidential, as is the case for therapists and clergy, or for employees who are required to share information with campus authorities.

These telling rules also apply to how institutional authorities listen. For instance, the faculty member designated as a responsible employee is instructed to interrupt a student to inform them that, as a mandatory reporter, anything they share will be reported to Title IX. The faculty member or office supervisor cannot listen attentively as the student's story unfolds,[7] as they gather the courage to speak the unspeakable. Rather, the responsible employee must be on alert for anything that suggests a telling might be forthcoming so that they can interject with a procedural caveat: "before you continue, I need you to know that I will have to share the details of your experience with Title IX." This technique, referred to as "interrupt to inform," can impact the student negatively if the student feels unheard or dismissed (Stone 2020). Words such as "I need to stop you before you say more" alter the relational dynamic by slamming the brakes on an intimate exchange charged with emotion, thus shifting the interactional context from empathic to transactional and procedural. In this way transactional rules seep into the community well beyond the Title IX office.

Confidentiality is certainly warranted and is intended to protect the survivor's identity, an important aim given the shame and blame associated with sexual assault. However, confidentiality usually translates into a form of secret keeping. Maintaining confidentiality of a particular case becomes a collective silence around sexual assault on campus writ large. Institutions practice avoidance by hiding behind the cloak of confidentiality; confidentiality justifies silence. However, confidentiality about a specific case does not mandate silence about an issue or excuse the college of its epistemic obligation, its responsibility to make knowledge about sexual violence available within the community.

Some of Title IX's listening rules, and by extension the college's listening rules, are implicit and undergird how the official reporting process is fundamentally transactional. Title IX policies require its officials to follow a listening guide, of sorts: Does the incident, as reported, and to the extent evidence supports it, conform to one or more preset categories of sexual misconduct, or not? Can someone on campus be held responsible? The teller has a story to share of relational betrayal; to tell an official of that experience is, at minimum, seeking to be heard and understood, and hopefully for justice or remedy. Listening to detect a priori particulars is not the same as virtuous listening, nor the same as the survivor being heard. The former involves openness to what the teller might say or needs to say. The one is transactional, the other relational.

What and How to Tell

A student who decides to share their experience with an institutional authority is placing trust in that person or office to execute college policies faithfully. Students and their allies approach Title IX trusting that the process will provide support and result in some action. Their trust carries the expectation that their telling will be deemed credible and that the institution will respond to the acquired knowledge. Students encounter a very different telling process with campus authorities than the one they have experienced with others. For the most part, students have already shared their experiences with friends or peers who are predisposed to trust based on their close ties. These thick relations do not require a specific speech performance by one party (Wanderer 2017) to establish credibility or require the listener to assume a neutral position that weighs competing claims. A peer who questions their claims would violate the thick relations of intimacy and acquaintance. In the previous chapter, we discussed the negative impact of friends questioning the survivor's account or actions. However, the structure of Title IX does just that; it asks questions, weighs competing evidence, and ascertains the credibility of the participants. Rather than trusting the survivor's words, the process adopts a skeptical stance until the evidence becomes "the weight of a feather" or as clear and compelling as a bruised body.[8]

The student's testimony, the "what" dictated by formal telling rules, must shapeshift into a stylized narrative form that fits a procedural frame for it to be deemed credible. The survivor's telling is pushed through an evaluative structure only to have their experience reinterpreted for them (Foucault 2019). No, what you experienced was not an assault, or yes, our investigation substantiates your claims that you were raped. Institutional authorities or experts, the interlocutors, determine intelligibility by stipulating what information about the incident is relevant or, in short, credible. They also determine what features of the telling transaction are most important, be they semantic conventions (i.e., what can be said or considered) or the performative context (i.e., how the teller and listeners comport themselves), all of which stand in stark contrast to a telling to a friend or confidant.

The Title IX process, the how, is designed to treat equally the participants on both sides, the complainant (survivor) and respondent (perpetrator). Impartial individuals investigate the survivor's testimony or telling, and the perpetrator has an opportunity to address the survivor's claims. Individuals often rely on the performance or delivery of a telling to gauge credibility, and those who have experienced significant trauma are expected to behave in specific ways. For instance, in a civil trial against Donald Trump, E. Jean Carroll, who has accused Donald Trump of raping her in a department store dressing room, was questioned about whether she called the police or told her family or if she showered, took medication for her bruised hand, or took pictures of her injuries. The media headline question was, "Why didn't she scream?"[9] Survivors are expected to display emotion, to be upset but not so much as to be viewed as hysterical or unhinged, to provide an account that outlines the details and is consistent over time (even though research documents the impact of trauma on memory), to preserve evidence but not so much so that it looks like they made up the rape as part of a revenge plot or, in the case of Carroll, a political plot.

Neurobiologists caution against performative expectations, and in recent years trauma-informed approaches have attempted to recalibrate these expectations. While acknowledging the neurobiology of trauma, the preamble to the 2020 Title IX regulations states that institutions may use trauma-informed approaches if they are part of an impartial, unbiased system. A college may not provide "training that instructs Title IX personnel to assume that complainants are always truthful when filing complaints, while respondents are always responsible for sexual harassment once accused." The preamble states that a college cannot train Title IX personnel "to scrutinize factual inconsistencies or errors more closely when offered by a respondent than a complainant." Colleges cannot discount the inconsistencies of the survivor, due to trauma, for example, and then use inconsistencies in the respondent's account to determine responsibility. Trauma-informed approaches are permissible, but as the regulations point out, applying them in an impartial, unbiased manner is challenging.

How the Title IX process assesses the survivor's credibility—whether officials can trust that they are telling the truth about their experience and that their definition of the incident matches legal definitions and what is specified in college policy—is under review. Under Title IX regulations, colleges and universities can opt to include the cross-examinations of both parties as part of the investigation.[10]

The telling structure is designed to protect institutional interests and to make sure that colleges respond and are "not deliberately indifferent" to sexual violence. As such, the process holds institutions accountable to a degree to ensure colleges and universities do not look the other way. It is an admirable goal and one that has been needed. However, under this structure, the institution's interests can be at odds with the interests of the student survivors and their confidants. Students encounter this tension when they realize the process assumes a position of neutrality, and their testimony must be found, rather than assumed to be, credible. Both parties begin the process on equal footing, thereby positioning the college outside of relationships. Students also encounter tension when they discern Title IX's implicit listening rules and, as well, when they are asked not to talk to others about their case.

The neutrality of Title IX diverges from the friend's or family member's obligation to trust the interpretation of the survivor. Intelligibility, as Medina (2013) contends, depends on the communicative framework and whether the telling is to oneself or sympathetic or unsympathetic others. The Title IX process is neither sympathetic nor unsympathetic, and this is where expectations and experience collide. The who, what, and how of the institution's telling/listening rules create relational tensions and impediments that jeopardize trust and perceptions of goodwill. These, in turn, reinforce the existent gaps, lacunae, and fractures in the institution's sexual violence awareness field.

Institutional Betrayal

Survivors and their confidants who report an assault trust that a college representative or official, upon the receipt of this information, will take up the matter and will be moved to act to restore a social order, a campus culture that decries sexual violence. Sometimes, the institutional process meets these expectations, survivors are provided needed support, and perpetrators are found responsible and sanctioned accordingly. Institutional betrayal occurs when a college fails to protect students from assault adequately or responds to a sexual assault report in a way that exacerbates the anxiety and trauma associated with the assault (Stone 2020). When the Title IX process does not go as expected, students (and staff) feel betrayed.

Institutional betrayal, as it applies to sexual assault, has been studied most often in terms of its impact on the emotional and mental health of survivors (Smith and Freyd 2013). We contend that institutional betrayal also has important implications for understanding the circulation of knowledge within the epistemological field. A sense of betrayal impedes the circulation of knowledge on campus, limiting the possibilities for knowledge uptake and acquisition. Stef expresses this sentiment: "I thought it was going to be okay if I told COLLEGE about it but this wasn't the case."

With trust, one does not expect the other party to take care of things just any way but in a particular way with a spirit of goodwill (Carter 2020). When a person trusts another, they make themselves vulnerable; they assume an attitude of good will, what philosophers call sincerity, and competence, that implies fulfilled expectation or action (Grasswick 2018). Survivors assume sincerity and competence from Title IX and expect the process to support them. They are shocked to encounter a "neutral" institutional structure. The neutrality of the process feels "unfair for the survivors of assault." Candance, a Black heteroflexible senior, says, "There isn't much space for survivors to take up. It seems like the space must be shared with violators and we have to be silenced. College makes the problems disappear as if it does not happen." Candance is correct. In recent years, Title IX has become a contested discursive space between the rights of survivors and the rights of those named as the assailants or perpetrators.

Colleges and universities have been cautioned to watch what they say and do or face legal action. The conflicting tension between the rights of survivors and the rights of those named in complaints often feels as if a process survivors thought would benefit them has been usurped by larger institutional and political interests. A few students were able to name these conflicting power interests. Aimee admits that although she has experienced an ethic of care among college administrators, seemingly a precursor to sincerity, there are conflicting interests: "The overwhelming number of administrators I talked to seem like they care but I cannot believe things are going to be handled seriously if the Title IX coordinator works for the school they are responsible to investigate. I believe that this is a major conflict of interest that could cloud the judgment of people that are supposed to help victims."

Survivors hope that the college will "do something" and that the action will be commensurate with the situation. Expected actions run the gamut from wanting an apology to needing accommodation for late academic work to hoping the perpetrator is expelled from the college. When a case does not go as the student expects, this knowledge circulates within the whisper network, too, and the institution's actions and lack thereof, more so than the well-intentioned efforts of officials, erode trustworthiness. The legacy of these Title IX histories persists, the damage lingering well beyond the tenure of specific persons (Grasswick 2018). Only 28 percent of students responding to the AAU climate survey indicated that it was very or extremely likely that the officials would do all of the following: take the report seriously, conduct a fair investigation, and take action to address the causes of the issue. Students do not have high expectations for college officials to act in ways supportive of students who have been assaulted.

When college officials act in ways counter to expectations, students feel "traumatized." Kiera, a student leader on campus, describes a scary encounter involving members of an athletic team. She reported the incident to Title IX and hoped they would take specific actions. She describes the incident and her expectations for how the college would respond:

> The X team were drinking in an off-campus apartment and began sending me sexually explicit and offensive text messages asking me for sexual favors in return for money as well as group sex. I turned off my phone and went to sleep. Three or more members of this group came to campus, into my dorm at around 1 A.M. banging on my door and shouting at me to let them in. I woke in a panic, terrified that my door was open. While they were banging and shouting, they sent me snapchats [videos] of them laughing and telling me they were going to rape me. They eventually left my room and went to the floor below mine and did the same thing to my friend. We filed an informal complaint with Title IX to deactivate their dorm cards and mandate they could not be enrolled in the same courses as us. I also requested a written apology (I wanted to file a formal complaint but was advised against because "it would take too long" and the school "wanted me and my friend to have immediate protection," which I think is bullshit). They were not otherwise penalized. Only two perpetrators were subjected to the process, and they were also allowed to make demands in the settlement (I was an RA at the time, and one of my harassers requested that I not perform my RA rounds in his building because I made HIM uncomfortable). Altogether the Title IX process was nearly as traumatizing as the actual event.

Kiera and her friends followed the process, thinking the college would take action to protect her and her friend. Although she had planned to file a formal complaint, a required step in finding a student responsible, she says she was discouraged from filing a complaint, the first instance in which her expectations were not met. When she found herself on the receiving end of a negative action, she felt betrayed by the process, adding that it was "nearly as traumatizing as the event."

Camila, a senior, expresses a similar sentiment following an assault that involved a person with whom she had had a consensual sexual relationship. She opted not to report the incident to Title IX due to its "ambiguous nature." Camila knew that her past relationship with the person might affect her credibility. She did tell others about the assault, and it was her telling others that prompted a Title IX response:

> We had been in a relationship where we had consensual sex regularly. He often asked for a verbal yes. At one point, I told him that stopping and asking me for a verbal yes was not always necessary, and I would tell him when I was uncomfortable with him proceeding. The night of the incident, I was visibly out of it, drunk, and gave no indication that I could consent. When I asked him to get

off of me after he penetrated my [limp] body, he left my room angrily and sent me a passive-aggressive text. I found this behavior disturbing and dangerous. I chose not to report due to the ambiguousness of the incident. I told the close friends around me what had happened, including some of his. Around a month later, I was called into the Title IX office and told he had filed a no-contact order against me. I was given no explanation as to why the order was filed. To this day I am traumatized by the way the situation was handled by Title IX, and that I could so easily have this order filed against me without explanation or without an offer for advocacy on the part of the Title IX office. I am not allowed to speak about what happened due to the order.

Camila did not follow the appropriate communicative channels for telling. When she violated a telling rule by talking about the assault to other students, Title IX acted against her without any offer of support. Both Camila and Kiera describe a situation in which they thought they would be the ones supported or offered advocacy. Instead, they found themselves on the other side as the students to be sanctioned. Both students were expecting a different response and outcome and were devastated and traumatized, to use their words, to find *their* actions, not those of their perpetrators, regulated.

The question of who benefits from Title IX processes surfaces in another context. Title IX is not designed to support all students who have experienced an assault. Federal regulations determine the conditions in which a survivor can seek services and/or disciplinary outcomes. According to Title IX regulations, a college is not required to respond to assaults that occur off campus in noncollege housing with nonenrolled students. For those students who have been assaulted off campus by nonstudents, there are fewer on-campus resources; they are encouraged to use community services such as the police and/or community counseling services, which may include local rape crisis centers. Cole was raped by someone she met on Tinder. When she described what happened to a friend on campus, the friend insisted she go to the hospital to get checked out. Cole describes the hours-long process at the hospital with the police and doctors as traumatic, particularly since "all of them didn't seem to believe me or weren't being understanding." As Cole learned, rape does not respect the boundaries of the campus in the same way that Title IX does. When the rape started to impact her academic performance, Cole reached out to the Title IX office: "This event caused me to fall behind in my classes and I was worried about my grades, so I reached out to Title IX to see if they could reach out to my professors for me to amend their attendance policy or arrange extensions or something because I had heard of this happening for other students. The Title IX coordinator told me there was basically nothing the office could do for me because the incident didn't involve another college student."

Cole was left to figure out how best to handle the situation independently. Cole's experience is not uncommon; other students, like Cole, who are assaulted off campus or at home during academic breaks do not fall within the purview of Title IX, even though the assault affects their college experience.[11] A survey of more than one hundred students who formally reported their assault found that nearly 40 percent who reported their assault to schools are pushed out of education. Of these students, 27 percent took a leave of absence, 20 percent transferred to another school, and nearly 10 percent dropped out (Advocates for Youth 2021).

Katie realized she had been raped only during a first-year orientation session on consent:

> Although I knew what happened that night was not typical, I didn't know enough about consent to label it as rape. It was during orientation when the first years attended consent workshops that I realized what had happened that night was indeed rape. Even with that realization, it took me about a year to start divulging this information to friends and identifying as a "survivor." I never went to Title IX about this incident because it happened off campus, with a noncollege-affiliated person, and I did not want to pursue a formal complaint. I did not avoid coming to Title IX out of distrust for the office— I just didn't think they could do anything to help me. Perhaps this was naive of me.

Katie didn't think Title IX could help her because her assault occurred off campus with a noncollege-affiliated person. Once she named what happened, it took time for her to make sense of it and share the experience with others. She did not report her rape to campus authorities because she did not think they could do anything—again, a reference to some expectation that a report produces some action. She adds that her decision was not a result of "distrust for the office," an elaboration that implies others, not her, might distrust the office.

Students are aware of Title IX, and while seeking support from the Title IX office generally increased across our surveys, satisfaction with the experience generally declined: only 35.3 percent of those in 2020 rated their overall Title IX experience positively, compared to 71.4 and 40.0 percent who did so in 2016 and 2018. In 2022, there were too few respondents to form an estimate. A declining sense of satisfaction with the office may signal questions about perceived trustworthiness.

The trust institutions elicit from community members is fragile and fraught, and once it is broken, it is harder to reestablish it than to create it in the first place (Code 2020). Kanesha, a Black bisexual student who had blacked out during the assault, reported the incident to Title IX only to regret the decision later: "The process that they put students through is the worst and an additional incident happened that resulted in me losing all trust in Title IX and the COLLEGE administration as a whole." Smith and Freyd (2013) find that sexual assault that occurs in a context in which the institution acts in a way that betrays trust is especially harmful and exacerbates the impact of the assault on the student.

Betrayal erodes the climate of trust, and a climate of trust is needed to nourish and sustain epistemological communities. When survivors and/or their friends mention their encounters with the Title IX office, their comments often identify aspects of the process linked to trust, either sincerity (how they are treated or made to feel) or competence (the actions taken or not taken). Stef's description of being made to feel "small" and Kiera's and Camila's surprise at finding the college was acting against them exemplify how sincerity and competence can be compromised during the process. A few students who were discouraged from filing a formal complaint describe feeling like the office brushed off or minimized their experience, which conveyed the implicit message that the incident was not serious enough to merit a closer examination of what occurred or to sanction the perpetrator. Becca says she "couldn't go through with Title IX because she felt so discouraged." Like Becca, Sasha describes similar obstacles to filing a formal complaint: "I have tried to report people, and the Title IX office has told me not to. Three of them were/are resident advisors on campus." Sasha's comments imply that leadership roles may confer advantages to some students. Both Becca and Sasha could not exercise their epistemic agency in ways they expected.

Stories about how the institution has responded to previous sexual assault cases are an influential part of the student discourse. When asked what she remembered most when her friend told her about the assault, her confidant responds, "Title IX didn't do shit." When students share stories and come into relational awareness that their experiences are endemic and normalized but not recognized, they feel dismayed, disheartened, and betrayed. Past failures exert a powerful effect on student decision-making. Shondra, a student of color, says, "Title IX at COLLEGE always had a bad rep so I never actually went to anyone at the office." Logan, a senior, offers a similar explanation for his decision-making: "I was groped after being emotionally manipulated by a student who trauma dumped on me and then claimed she couldn't fall asleep without someone else in the room, and I felt bad so I went over. I did not ask to be touched in the way she did . . . was very inappropriate. I didn't report because the Title IX department sucks and has been extremely unhelpful to my other survivor friends." Logan draws on testimonial knowledge from other survivors as part of his decision not to report to Title IX. Jade, who identifies as queer, forms their epistemological community with a fellow survivor in response to the treatment they received from Title IX: "She and I were both enduring excruciating experiences with Title IX and found each other through a mutual friend, who asked if we would be interested in speaking with someone who had a similar

experience to us. Our friendship formed out of mutual sharing of our experience with COLLEGE's rape culture and unprofessional/generally horrible
Title IX office." Stories of negative encounters with college officials and offices
seep into the whisper networks and circulate along those relational paths. These
narratives become part of the representational institutional story told about
campus sexual assault. These narratives shape how students perceive the institution: "COLLEGE does nothing when it comes to sexual assault. I don't feel safe. I
don't like COLLEGE anymore."

Conclusion

Individuals and communities depend on one another for knowledge, and this
interdependence is necessary for an equitable circulation of knowledge within
the epistemic field. Colleges rely on students to provide them with the "actual
knowledge" they need in order to respond to sexual assault.[12] Survivors who
report to Title IX or other college officials are exercising their epistemic agency
in their capacity as knowers, and college administrators or responsible employees who are on the receiving end of students' attempts to convey their experience are also exercising epistemic agency in their capacity to receive this
knowledge and to act based on it. Both parties, the speaker and the hearer, trust
the other. Unfortunately, the structure purportedly designed to increase institutional knowledge and protect students strips away what the college most
needs to know. Sensing the college would rather not know, that the college is
not inclined to listen, the students who could tell them, who perhaps already
tried to tell them feel betrayed, and come to believe the college is untrustworthy.
This pall of distrust rests on top of the largely invisible epistemic triad.

More broadly, the Title IX process, with its associated telling/listening rules,
has the effect, perhaps unintended, of tamping down voices about sexual violence by rendering them into propositions and routing them along official dead-
end channels that require confidentiality. Formal telling rules neutralize the
disruptive potential of tellings and reclaim them as part of a strategy of recuperation (Alcoff and Gray 1993) instead of strategies of community understanding and transformative justice. Speech that can't be silenced is channeled into
nonthreatening outlets, confessionals of sorts, that very few people can talk
about and that the institution can manage and regulate.[13] Students who violate these formal telling rules are sanctioned. When survivors' telling is discred-
ited and/or their experience is defined as inconclusive, or they are sanctioned
for violating formal telling rules, their epistemic subjectivity and their ability
to know their own experience is damaged or even erased (Code 2014). It is not
unusual to hear survivors describe the process as retraumatizing. Often, students feel the institution has betrayed them. When students experience the
institutional process as harmful and retraumatizing, to use their words, this

knowledge seeps back into the whisper network, eroding student trust in the college's ability to act ethically and justly and shaping how students perceive institutional trustworthiness and integrity.

By formally routing tellings along particular communication channels, ones shrouded in secrecy and confidentiality, the institution remains in control of the circulation of knowledge of assault, at least within the commons or officialdom, ensuring not knowing and wanting to not know will persist up and down and across the college community. What students could say about "what is really happening" is mainly unrecognized, and, in any event, unwelcomed officially. Although sexual violence has long been a tightly held secret, with the implementation of the guidelines that formalize telling rules, sexual assault has become the best-kept open secret on campus, with an institutional structure in place to protect the secret.

Conclusion

Having Heard Their Stories

> We are not complaining. We are not begging. We are not yelling. We are simply telling. Telling others the stories that we have held inside of us for too long. Stories that we should have been told by our mothers, our sisters, our friends. Stories that I hope my daughter never has to tell me. The only way we can educate people on the subject of rape is by telling these stories.
>
> —*Hear My Voice*

Delving into the Gap

Recall that the impetus for this research emerged from a small group of students concerned about the mismatch between what they knew as students and what campus security and college administrators knew as the record keepers of student conduct violations. In the language of our research, they were asking how institutional authorities could be avoiders. Like other student activists, they were perplexed by the recurring need to remind college officials and some of their peers that assaults happen on and off this campus and to students in the community with regularity, and many students, not only those who have been assaulted, are impacted academically and psychologically as a result. How could the college not know? Why wouldn't it actively seek this knowledge?

Why was the institution silent about the occurrence of sexual violence in the community instead of speaking about it with regularity and urgency? Given academe's fundamental purpose, how can an "elephant in the quad" and the rule of thirds persist unacknowledged?

Our students' determination to document the vertical gaps between student and institutional knowledge was the kindling, the epistemic friction, needed to ignite our questions. In the process of trying to understand better why this vertical gap exists—why official knowledge and community knowledge are at odds—we encountered other knowledge gaps and deep ruts that create an uneven knowledge field around sexual assault that limits knowing and protects the status quo.

When we began our research, we didn't have a language for naming the various gaps or a conceptual framework for examining their connectedness and meaning. We didn't fully appreciate the impact of assault on the college community, how sexual assault and sexual violence reverberate invisibly up and down and across the community through a variety of relational networks, creating misunderstandings and community fractures. We didn't recognize that an expansive sense of betrayal is a feature of the fractures, and we were unaware of the structured, epistemic field in academia and its complicity in the damage. Focused as we were on incidents and how they affected students, we were unaware of the community's woundedness and the community's complicity.

These are some of the complexities and features of the epistemic field that we found difficult to consider without first conceiving the field itself, the "ether" within which the patterns arise. The complex architecture of gaps and channels, the whisperings and silencings, shroud within-community sexual assault as rumor or hearsay and as occasional, isolated transgressions, if not simply lapses in judgment. That sexual assault is a serious problem on campus is, even now, not deemed credible even while it is the best-kept open secret on campus. This is a betrayal of the community by the community itself.

Viewing an institution's epistemic field from above, seeing it as a structure shaped both by distant, seismic forces, such as tremors in the social imaginary and federal governing bodies, and by local proclivities, such as the institution's demographics, evolving policies, and onboarding curricula, invites us to consider the field itself, and what the whole structure eclipses. Some epistemic gaps, for example, seem neither horizontal nor vertical; they seem to run deeper, underpinning the field itself, manifesting as informational voids: concepts not yet conceived, language not yet adequate, questions not yet asked or askable, data not tracked, patterns not surmised. Consider, for example, the impact of Hall and Sandler's (1982) description of campus climate as "a chilly one for women" and the related, slow rise of the concept and term "sexual harassment," as namings of something previously experienced, certainly, but not yet conceived as a thing, with a name—something that could be studied and tracked, even prevented.

Until we administered the 2020 survey, we, like most researchers, asked follow-up questions about only one form of telling: reporting. Moreover, we asked no questions of those who hold this knowledge as trusted confidants, firsthand witnesses to the survivor's story. It's as if tremulous knowledge within the undercommons—relational knowledge—was not considered: not thought about, not relevant to the problem, not deemed of value, not even considered knowledge. Even with the well-intentioned efforts to acquire this knowledge through climate surveys, what is deemed relevant bends to the perspective of those with the power to shape and define. Krause et al. (2019) found that of the 107 climate surveys administered at 101 schools, only 35 percent of reports covered all six topics outlined by "Not Alone" (The White House Task Force to Protect Students from Sexual Assault 2014).[1] Even when all recommended questions are asked, the questions asked of students skew information in certain ways. This channeling hews to unacknowledged contours of the knowledge field as it communicates what's important or valued in the dominant discourse. Knowledge is often the making of the powerful, reflecting their experiences and beliefs, what they deem important. As such, members of marginalized groups often can best see the distortions, the blind spots, the gaps, and whose interests they serve. Students could see what we could not initially.[2] We are confident that students at other colleges and universities possess the type of lucidity (Medina 2013) that can address knowledge lacunae by pointing out what's missing, what's distorted, and what's simply wrong.

The discursive silence around sexual assault on college campuses has less to do with the actions of survivors and their confidants and more to do with a structure designed to manage tellings. We have argued that that structure ensures overreliance on a fundamentally nonrelational way of knowing. There are many tellings. Survivors do tell others, and relatively soon after an experience. To a much lesser extent, confidants also tell others, but usually to those outside their local networks. Rather than an absence of discourse, the discourse on campus is very private, channeled, and contained. Only if and when the discourse becomes disembodied and transformed into propositional knowledge is it allowed to be shared, and even then, it seldom springs into community-wide awareness, let alone community-wide conversation. As our research shows, persistent, harmful, within-community knowledge gaps or lacunae are intrinsic to the epistemic field of campus sexual assault.

The Epistemic Field of Campus Sexual Assault

We have tried to build a useful conceptual model of the discursive dynamics of a community living the rule of thirds, having normalized the occurrence of sexual assault and somehow having agreed, for the most part, not to talk about it publicly. As described, campus tellings move through a structure that governs how knowledge is produced, acquired, and circulated. This structure, called the epistemic field, regulates the who, what, when, and how of telling. Formal and informal telling rules apply to both tellers and listeners and govern who acquires knowledge, how and when the knowledge is shared or circulated, and the content conveyed to audiences.

Student Awareness

The field's lateral unevenness gives rise to differently situated networks of student knowers, some who know about sexual assault through experience and/or a telling from a friend or student, and some who have, by privilege, avoided acquiring this knowledge, either actively, by deliberate actions on their part, or passively, because of limited exposure to the community, or both. A student's position in the epistemic triptych influences how they perceive the overall campus climate and the institution's responsiveness to campus assaults. Goffman (1963, 42) describes how asymmetries in knowledge "divide the world into the wise and naive." Our findings show that those who know-with view the institution less favorably and are more likely to question the college's ability to respond to sexual assault fairly and equitably. This specific knowledge seeps into the institutional groundwater, contaminating one's views and perspectives of one's college experience.

Avoiders, those students who have not been assaulted and know no other students who have, are more likely to see the college through rose-colored glasses. They are less likely than students who know someone or those assaulted to think sexual assault is a problem, and they have more confidence that the institution will respond appropriately, with fairness, trust, and compassion. Their sanguine views are fraught, given that time and exposure to others increase the odds that they will acquire this knowledge through experience and/or peer telling. Sustained avoidance requires effort and diligence to maintain the comfort of not knowing or needing not to know. Avoidance manifests as a difficulty seeing oneself as affected by a problem—the white person who struggles to understand racism or the man who does not need to think about reproductive rights. This distancing of self is harder when the concern involves someone you know, someone with whom you have close affective ties.

For most of the student population who have acquired relational knowledge about sexual assault, this knowledge does more than impact their attitudes and perspectives; it leaves a scar. Our findings demonstrate the impact of an assault on the survivor and, of significance, the impact of the assault on those who occupy the status of confidant, those who know via tellings. Our data visualizations allow us to see how confidants pick up and carry the pain of sexual assault for their friends. The wounds they carry, while not as deep as survivors', are invisible in the college community and in the research literature. On some measures, the impact approximates the impact of those who have experienced assault but have not told anyone, at least yet.

As heavy as this relational knowledge can be, it also has the power to transform. Those who possess this knowledge show greater capacity for empathy and action. Knowing-with affects how students relate to each other and the institution, disrupting privileged ways of knowing and filling in cognitive and affective lacunae.

What have we learned about tellings from students who hold this relational knowledge? Most students in the epistemic field are secret keepers, those survivors and friends who can only whisper with one another about their experiences. Our qualitative data explore the meanings associated with telling a confidant. Far from being a transmission of information, tellings are co-constructed meaning-making endeavors. The reaction of the confidant to the telling shapes how survivors make sense of their experience and whether others can be trusted to hear what they tell in all its complexity, confusion, pain, and vulnerability. Relational norms of friendship dictate how one listens to the telling, and confidants feel obligated to honor these telling rules as a performative display of friendship.

The epistemic field among students also encompasses a group of silence holders, students who have been assaulted but have told no one. What is striking about this group is their connection to the whisper network. Only a few silence holders reside outside the whisper network and are genuinely isolated from others with a similar experience. By far, most silence holders have been told by others. Their decision to not share their experience with others, although they did share it with us, points to their wariness of the campus climate. Perhaps they have been burned when they previously shared something private; perhaps there are no conceptual categories that can hold their experience; perhaps they have bowed under the resignation that the world can be a cruel place for women and nonbinary or genderqueer persons. They are far from naive about the consequences of telling.

Other Gaps and Lacunae

We have not explored a sizable portion of the epistemic field: the networks among administrators, faculty, and staff. It is logically certain that among the nonstudent groups within the college community, be they faculty, administrators, or staff, some are unaware of sexual assault within the community, others are aware, and some of those who are aware have experienced it personally. Their awareness or lack thereof might be about sexual assault experienced by students, or it might be about sexual assault experienced by employees at the school, such as would be the case if some faculty knew of other faculty whom another community member had assaulted. We did not survey faculty, staff, or administrators about their personal awareness of within-community sexual violence.

Consequently, we cannot empirically map how relational knowledge of sexual violence is distributed up and down the institution's hierarchy, nor how it moves laterally and vertically within and across those groups. We suspect they would fall into similar groupings, but we leave it to future researchers to answer this question. That said, neither of us is an "avoider" as such because, unfortunately, we are all too aware of instances of sexual misconduct among nonstudent groups. Over the years, we have sometimes found ourselves included in their various whisper networks when colleagues have shared their own stories with us. We, too, have felt the obligation to maintain their confidence and to abide by nondisclosure agreements. We acknowledge that this important aspect of the community's epistemic field remains unmapped and that it would be an interesting line of inquiry with representative stories worth telling.

Institutional Avoidance

We foreground the stories of students, both survivors and their confidants, to understand better how and why local, within-community sexual assault awareness can be so uneven across the community. Their whispered stories are shaped by and reveal the epistemic field. However, their stories are not the only ones impacted by the nature and structure of the field. Within the past decade, institutions have become part of the narrative about campus sexual assault, and their emergent role in the discourse is an important aspect of the representational story. Institutions are now expected to be open to "knowing that" a sexual assault has occurred within the student community and to take appropriate action. They have long resisted even this limited type of knowing and have slowly moved away from considering assaults to be rare, singular, and a strictly carceral matter, best left to the police and criminal justice system. This development, in the service of ensuring educational equity, is an important, positive change.

Imagine how different the campus culture has become from the time, not so long ago, when there were no college policies that prohibited certain forms of sexual violence and there were no offices tasked with responding to sexual assault on campus. That there is institutional knowledge even of this limited kind and that there are now institutional stories that can be told about coming into this awareness are consequential. However, this type of institutional knowledge has not produced the community uptake needed to create transformational change and deepen students' trust in college leaders. Why?

Not Needing to Know

Colleges and universities have engaged in their own avoidance dance. Institutional avoidance has taken different forms over the decades, often a potent combination of passive ignorance—we can't be held responsible for things we do not know—and active ignorance—we won't inquire or talk about or hear those things we do not want to know. Though researchers have documented the prevalence of sexual assault of college students for decades,[3] colleges and universities have not been required or expected to know about its presence on campus, and when they do know, to know only some of its features. In this century, thanks to the federal government, colleges in the United States are required to know about sexual assault, and a college that knows is responsible for investigating incidents to determine what occurred and the steps needed to resolve the situation.[4] We see this as a step forward, one not to be dismissed, even as we recognize its limitations, including the ease with which this knowledge is used as political fodder and how the federal resolve to know is subject to erasure.

The persistent meta-blindness of colleges and universities to the prevalence of sexual assault on their campuses and how its effects harm the entire community speaks to the resilience of the epistemic field.[5] Before the broadening of Title IX, institutions could not be held responsible for those things they did not know. If students did not report their assaults, college officials were off the hook for knowing. In the past, it was easier for institutions to sidestep their ethical obligations by claiming passive ignorance. Of course, they did not think to ask students, either. Perhaps they did not know how to ask about it or feared it was too sensitive or private a topic to broach with students, best left to hang in the campus ether until someone brings it up. Before impugning institutional leaders for willful neglect, though that may be the case in some institutions, it is worth remembering and acknowledging that everyone, including our institutions, has blind spots. Medina (2013) cautions that we cannot expect individuals and institutional leaders to be open to, a priori, let alone relationally connected to disturbing information when there is a history and constellation of social practices designed to block or limit it.

In response to these external pressures and concerns about federal sanctions and student lawsuits, colleges and universities have introduced generic and policy-laden information about sexual assault and misconduct that has provided "off-the-shelves" epistemic resources (Bailey 2014) shared during orientation or onboarding. They have hired Title IX staff and created and clarified reporting procedures. A cottage industry of Title IX professionals has emerged to help institutions keep up with changing regulations, minimize risks, and ensure compliance. These processes and policies are designed to make sure tellings are funneled to administrative offices tapped with providing survivor support and responding to sexual assault complaints. Initially, these changes seemed like promising efforts that would increase institutional knowledge and provide student support, maybe even reduce the occurrence of sexual assault.

These recent institutional changes reflect the dominant perspective that the epistemic "problem" of sexual assault requires an organizational fix. By this reasoning, institutional avoidance results from inefficiencies in the epistemic system, not a problem with the system itself (Dotson 2014; Bailey 2014). Based on this logic, college officials do not know because students are not telling them, and students are not telling them because they do not know how to report an assault. Enhanced propositional and procedural knowledge, how college policies define assault and related prohibitions and what procedures to follow if assaulted (or told of an assault), should reduce these inefficiencies. This information, often shared during orientation, fills essential information gaps, if absorbed, and it undoubtedly has helped students. Colleges measure this type of knowledge—whether students know about the Title IX office, the reporting procedures if assaulted, and so on—to gauge "knowledge about sexual assault," which is how informed students are about policies, definitions, procedures, and resources. Similar training and checks are in place for employees. As we have shown and is consistent with findings at other colleges and universities, student awareness of policies, definitions, procedures, and resources has increased, and more students are using the available resources. This approach assumes this is the onboarding information and knowledge gaps that matter most when it comes to responding to sexual violence in academia and addressing institutional responsibility. These institutional responses probably are what matter most when it comes to institutions' legal exposure. As such, they stand tall in onboarding curricula. Institutions' moral exposure is a different matter.

The emphasis on Title IX processes exemplifies what Dotson (2014) calls a first-order epistemic change. The problem results from an inefficiency in the system—procedures for reporting need to be made more transparent, and students need to understand how to report an assault. The aim is to route more tellings into official channels within the epistemic field so college leaders can respond and support. Our data suggest, however, that despite these increased efforts, most students are still not telling college administrators about their experiences, and students have good reasons for not engaging in the process. This organizational change fails to see how the problem is the epistemic field itself. In this field, the knowledge that matters most, relational knowledge, the knowing-with that moves through the student community, is not what counts, quite literally. Moreover, these changes miss what students identify as the obstacles that stand in the way of their telling.

As a result of focusing on first-order epistemic changes, the true nature of the problem is veiled, and the community, consequently, need not see, acknowledge, or contend with its wounds nor its complicity. The information disseminated in college orientations and policy brochures cannot account for the most disturbing within-community blind spots or lacunae or the unlevel knowledge field within which those lacunae reside. That the pervasiveness of sexual assault and misconduct within the student community and how students experience them are pointedly not discussed in the sexual misconduct onboarding orientations, nor included anywhere within the institution's curriculum, signifies how one can know-of, know-that, and know-how without knowing with the community.

These practices, whether tacit or inscribed in policies, serve as institutional meaning-making frames. When students who have been assaulted are directed to whom they should report their experiences and how to report, their stories are truncated, shaped, and distorted; relational knowledge is filtered and discarded. These channels are designed to codify, adjudicate, and hence transform relational knowledge into bite-size nuggets of information. The knowledge that moves from the undercommons into the commons passes through an institutional sieve, most often connected to the Title IX office, that strains out portions of the experience, the affective and relational particulates unrelated to determining responsibility. Anita Hill understands what it means to have a telling contorted to fit a particular narrative: "When we are not allowed to tell in our words what is happening, when we have to go through an interrogator, we are missing the full story. Moreover, we fail to capture the full story, we miss the chance to make lasting change" (as quoted by Yarinsky 2018). The template for the Title IX complaint organizes the story (Bruner 2003), and this story differs from a community story. A structure designed to determine individual responsibility for community infractions is not suited for creating shared knowledge.

The knowledge that emerges on the other side, called "official or actual knowledge" by the federal government, is converted into transactional knowledge. Only when a telling is reported to and validated by a college authority does it become official or actual knowledge; only then does an institution "know" about sexual assault. These pathways have the effect, intended or not, of restricting what is to be known, who is to know, and the interpretive resources available within the community and for the community. By limiting what constitutes official knowledge, whom it affects, and how knowledge is conveyed and acquired, institutions have maintained their ignorance and minimized their responsibility (and liability).

Given that the only knowledge that counts as "actual" knowledge is the knowledge that moves from the whisper networks into formal administrative channels, incidents that occur outside of formal reporting channels remain primarily invisible: the late-night tellings, the impromptu confessions, the whispered "me toos" rendered inaudible to those in positions of power and withheld from public forums and discussions. Colleges and universities do not need to know what is whispered about in this epistemic system. Since these tellings fall outside the knowledge realm, students cannot claim epistemic agency within this epistemic structure. Why does this matter?

The inequitable distribution and circulation of relational knowledge and understanding around sexual assault on college campuses, including the communicative practices that impact its "uptake," constitute what Fricker (2007) and others (Medina 2013, 2017, 2018; Anderson 2012; Alcoff 2018) call epistemic injustice. Philosophers describe the injustices that arise when one's testimony is dismissed, minimized, or rejected due to the hearer's prejudice. Persons of color are all too familiar with the ease with which their experiences of racism or xenophobia are dismissed or minimized. Women know how it feels to have their experiences of harassment redefined as a misunderstanding. Philosophers also describe the epistemic injustices that occur when one's experience does not conform to existing categories; for example, the problem with no name, or when persons are unable to participate in the pooling and community uptake of information because the process excludes what they know—the confidants who are silent witnesses to their friend's pain (Anderson 2017). Students feel unheard and wronged in their capacity as knowers.

Victims/survivors often name these injustices as doubt, shame, and blame, and the situations that defy categorization as ambiguous—not this, but also not okay. The system asks survivors to carry the weight of their knowledge, to be heroic warriors in isolation. Confidants are shadow figures in the field. Though they are allowed to play a role as behavioral bystanders, reading situations and encounters as potentially harmful and intervening to thwart a possible sexual assault, these friends and peers are not accorded a space to act as epistemic bystanders—those folks who possess extensive knowledge of what is happening within their networks. Epistemic injustice is thus "built into the very structure of communicative practices, and . . . people can be hermeneutically disadvantaged in unfair ways even when we can't point to persons acting in ways that are identifiably wrong" (Medina 2017, 42). It is a system that favors not needing to know or needing to not know, and many students distrust it and feel betrayed by it.

Students understand the difference between not needing to know and needing to not know. What the students mention when they talk about institutional betrayal falls into the category of needing to not know about how sexual violence affects their community. Colleges and universities have acted, but not in a way that levels the epistemological field by increasing the circulation of knowledge, fulfilling students' expectations, or establishing a standard of ethical responsibility.

Needing to Not Know

The narrative that institutional avoidance results from passive ignorance caused by process inefficiencies is neither complete nor accurate. For decades, tellings have erupted into the commons, unmanaged and unmitigated.[6] Students, not administrators, have been the ones to question whether there might be more to the epistemological gap between the undercommons and the commons, to pervasive institutional avoidance, than simply a lack of information, an inefficiency. As a student writes in *Hear My Voice*, "Voices unwanted are voices unheard." Students have organized Take Backs the Nights and other Speak Outs, year after year. How does a college maintain its avoidant gaze while managing ruptures of this sort and claiming they do not know?

Avoidance, which scholars often call ignorance, represents more than what is unknown—a deficit or emptiness to be filled. Ignorance is attached to structures that perpetuate it through disinformation, apathy, censorship, secrecy, collective amnesia or forgetfulness, and selective perception or choice—for example, look here and not there, ask these questions, not those (see Proctor and Schiebinger 2008; Applebaum 2015). Privacy and confidentiality often translate into secrecy, even though they are not reducible to one another. One can tell without violating confidentiality—that has been our aim here. Without tellings, it is easy to fall into a state of collective amnesia until the next crisis or uprising.

Student resistance has often adopted more subversive tactics to make their voices heard. They violate telling rules in ways that force institutions to respond. The students who demonstrate outside administrative buildings, who write on bathroom walls or circulate spreadsheets of faculty to avoid, or who make a symbolic gesture by taping Athena's mouth on Columbia University's campus, or who tape their mouths as is the case in the Silent Protests on South African university campuses have realized that sometimes they must break the telling rules to be heard.

Tellings are powerful because they disrupt the grand narrative or, in Foucault's terms, the power/knowledge regime. Institutions respond swiftly to those tellings that erupt unexpectedly into the commons outside of sanctioned channels. They confiscate flyers that name a perpetrator and then demonstrably punish the authors. Sometimes, they simply tolerate, with carefully constructed public relations counternarratives, incidents they cannot control, such as redefining an act of resistance that involves carrying a mattress around on one's back to protest how the institution handled their sexual assault case into a public-facing student art project. Other times, they can count on an inattentive or disinterested community, wherein the eruption is short-lived and has no discernible effect on the epistemological field. Due to their disruptive capacity—their relationally, epistemically provocative, and disturbing nature—tellings are regulated: channeled, contained, rendered, and restricted to discursive forms such as the secret so that they can be forgotten or rendered hearsay.

However, what if these tellings are needed to create epistemic friction and generate uptake? For any academic community to contend and contest sexual assault and misconduct, it would have to permit a more natural flow of discourse, releasing, somehow, community members from their implicit vows of silence and secrecy, including lessening the community's (and culture's) strictures about telling. The strictures, remember, were designed to muffle and route so that the community at large can maintain its state of not knowing, not acknowledging, and hence mask its complicity. The routing of tellings along specific pathways that limit circulation harms a community's knowledge system by preventing it from being as extensive as it could be by restricting epistemic resources, excluding contributions, and withholding opportunities for epistemological development. Official, anonymous, and individualized "telling-ons" (such as those through Title IX) restrict collateral knowing (a flow of knowing-with), and they serve (and the process serves) to minimize within-community epistemic friction. Moreover, that, in turn, favors the status quo. The pool of publicly shared beliefs is smaller, allowing biases and perspectival narrowness to flourish and avoidance to take root (Daukas 2020).

Remaking the Epistemic Field of Sexual Assault: Imagining the Possibilities

> Liberation is always in part a story telling process: breaking stories, breaking silences, making new stories. A free person tells her own story. A valued person lives in a society in which her story has a place. (Solnit 2017, 19)

Being mindful of knowledge gaps is the raison d'être of colleges and universities. Each discipline, including ours, sociology and psychology, addresses gaps in knowledge and understanding and creates scaffolded curricula to usher students into the higher reaches of what is known and not yet known and how to observe, question, and know well. Each college and university oversees and regulates its academic community as a holistic educational entity. Like the various disciplines it houses, the university is mindful of knowledge gaps and marshals select curricular and extracurricular opportunities and pathways to guide students into general and specialized knowledge. Filling or bridging those gaps is considered essential. Colleges and universities can lean into their epistemic responsibilities to their students and communities to model the openness, or what Medina calls the "meta-lucidity" (2013), associated with seeking that of which they are yet unaware, or in other words, those illusive truths that await good questions.

Indicators of Change

What would it mean for an institution to model this type of meta-lucidity and to know with their students, not merely know of students assaulted? What would it mean for knowledge to flow more freely, expanding the opportunities for avoiders to encounter the epistemic friction needed to acquire knowledge that moves them to action? First, institutions can know only to the extent that the people in the institution know. If information is sequestered through Title IX procedures or nondisclosure agreements or rendered meaningless through aggregated statistical reports, such as Clery reports or climate surveys, that are not discussed by the community, then "knowing" is performative, a surface-level knowing that does not stick. Are colleges and universities open to acquiring knowledge beyond what federal or state governments require? The knowledge trickling into administrative spaces where it goes to die is hardly known. Knowing-with requires the kind of deep, vulnerable learning that is hard, uncomfortable, and often the product of failed attempts. It can be awkward, but we must be undeterred by our mistakes.

What would indicate that an institution knows more thoroughly and is open to it? What would be the tells? Indeed, the student and staff onboarding processes and materials would be different. The curriculum and training would include more than generic off-the-shelf epistemic resources. These resources would be tailored to the specific college or university community, calling attention to the sexual violence that occurs right there, within their community, and to its impact on the community. Institutional responses must target more than individual survivors, given how harm reverberates outward to encompass the community. Furthermore, most importantly, these responses would challenge the community to do better; compass-like, they would point the way forward.

There would be opportunities for community members to share their stories so that knowledge-of is always tethered to knowledge-with. These tellings might take the form of a first-person narrative. However, they could also be conveyed and represented by means of artistic and literary expressions and performative arts, such as Boalian improvisations.[7] Confidentiality and privacy would not be at odds with telling. These opportunities would not be one-offs but regular occurrences that create the conditions that Solnit's epigraph identifies: the freedom to tell one's story and the conditions for it to be honored. The latter brings relationality and virtuousness to the imperative of listening/talking. As we are all too aware now, there is abundant talking in higher education and American culture sans virtuous listening. Some higher education institutions are more explicit about teaching intergroup dialogue, of which virtuous listening must be a part. Recall that trust has an affective side; feeling heard and validated builds trust. Trust widens our capacities as knowers and deepens our epistemological responsibilities (Grasswick 2017).

Another institutional tell would be structured discursive spaces inviting the whisper networks to share their deep knowledge. The knowledge of confidants, our epistemic first responders, would be acknowledged and valued. Too often, survivors have been the ones to carry the burden of telling, in large part because the prevailing narrative has been the story of "what happened to me" (followed by "how I have healed"), which may be the narrative of a legal or administrative adjudicative frame or a therapeutic frame. However, it is not the only narrative and not a narrative that can repair a community's wound, even while it might foster individual healing. Other researchers (Hirsch and Khan 2020) have also emphasized the need for educational communities to act more proactively and think more systematically about those friends and peers in the community impacted by a friend's sexual assault. Justice asks something of the community; it asks the community to intervene, to show repentance, and to do what is necessary to make amends (Herman 2023). This is not a task (nor should it be) that survivors take on alone; it is a task, Herman (2023) contends, that draws on the commitment of an ethical community.

Echoability

Another tell is more subtle. Courageous individuals who risk much by telling their stories need their networks for amplification. Heroic performances, such as the student's testimony during a Take Back the Night or Kali's story of her rape, depend on networks that echo the performance—hence why whisper networks are essential. Without this network, survivors fall prey to heroic individualism, as we see by those silence holders who report they can handle it on their own or that they should get on with it. Medina (2013) uses Rosa Parks's case to illustrate how echoing and echoability are yoked. The popular story about Rosa Parks is one of heroic individualism, but the actual context is one of an individual operating within a network.[8]

Medina's two related concepts, "echoing" and "echoability," elucidate how social change occurs and refute overly simplified accounts that focus too much on individuals engaging in dramatic and courageous acts. As Medina (2013, 187) explains, "The transformative impact of performance that we consider heroic is crucially dependent on social networks and daily practices that echo that performance." When acts of resistance are not isolated but linked through social networks, these acts become echoable, and the chained actions of individuals and groups are more likely to generate the uptake needed to bring about change. We see this possibility in our research findings. Students who know others score higher on the empathy and activism scale. Knowing with others is transformative. Without networks, personal knowledge cannot gather the momentum needed to become social knowledge. Social knowledge is needed to spur action and create lasting change. When we think of the epistemic agent as an individual, it is hard to understand how communities experience epistemic injustice and how these communities engage in resistance (McHugh 2017).

Recent movements, such as #MeToo, show how others echo an individual's heroic action and create the foundation for a social movement. In their book, *She Said: Breaking the Sexual Harassment Story That Helped Ignite a Movement,*

Kantor and Twohey (2020) tell the stories of the many survivors and witnesses to Harvey Weinstein's decades of sexual exploitation and assault at Miramax Films who found the courage to tell their stories publicly.[9] Doing so invoked public tellings, accusations, and workplace changes. Many more survivors came forward, and Weinstein was eventually convicted and, as of this writing, is serving time in prison. This tribute to the power of telling is not meant to pressure or criticize anyone for choosing silence or secrecy. There are so many reasons why such choices can make sense, not least of all that it is their choice. However, it is to say that tellings, and even the possibility of telling, contain seeds of emancipation for survivors and their communities.[10]

Institutional knowing (truly knowing) would be an open or unrestricted kind of knowing-with, open to tellings that would challenge previous stasis. To contend and contest meaningfully, the community must come into knowing. The foundation of that coming into knowing is support for survivors and their confidants' coming into critical awareness—which is to say, coming into narratives of their experiences, rich in context and representativeness, with an eager, empathic, imaginative, listening community.[11] This would be a big tell.

Realizing this transformative potential at the community level is not a given but a discursive accomplishment that takes work and courage. It also requires persistence. As we have seen with the expansion of Title IX, inviting even the most limited versions of tellings into discourse can create new opportunities for discipline and normalization. Speech that is circumscribed within legitimate venues and acceptable frames, hence, ferried away from the commons, is stripped of its epistemically disruptive potential. Even best practices risk being recast in ways that reinscribe power and privilege. Knowing requires ongoing effort and a structure alert to its meta-blindness, to the new and ever-changing sites of its ignorance.

We hope that tellings, such as the ones shared in this book, can begin to move us all toward a more inclusive community story, one capable of holding the collective we: survivors and confidants, students and college leaders. Because tellings are interactional accomplishments imbued with expectation—what will you do or not do with this thing I have shared—they elicit a sense of moral and political responsibility. Tellings can empower survivors and their confidants as an enactment of constructive agency and a new formation of assertive subjectivity (Alcoff 2018) under the right conditions. That said, it is important to recognize risks: they can have the opposite effect, as we know all too well. South Africa's Truth and Reconciliation Commission (TRC) offers an example of a touted community-level model that foregrounds tellings, but its designers were unaware of their gendered blind spots. The TRC excluded much of women's experiences and definitions of what constitutes a gross violation of human rights (DeLaet and Mills 2018). Out of the over twenty thousand testimonies submitted, fewer than 1 percent mentioned sexual violence. In concluding statements, the TRC acknowledged its blindness to the types of abuse women experienced (South Africa TRC 1998). Without a well-tilled epistemic field, tellings will not encounter the conditions that facilitate uptake. With the right conditions, tellings have the potential to remake the community.[12]

We began this project by imagining what it would mean for the community to reckon with sexual assault on its campus: to see the community's wound and to constantly seek to do so, and to talk about it honestly, sensitively as a just and caring community dedicated not only to educational equity but to equity education. Stories of assault and other manifestations of gendered power-over dynamics within the community would be welcomed because power-over dynamics would be studied and contested within the very being of the institution's educational mission. Each story told—each telling—once it became tellable as a story, would be at once unique, a case unto itself, and simultaneously representative of something larger needing to be known, understood, and acted upon. In our research and in our time as teachers, mentors, and advocates for equity, we have seen glimpses of this kind of expansive storytelling: we have borne witness to many tellings and emergent stories and individuals and small groups grappling with multiple stories, trying to make the connections necessary for each story to hold the representative story, and, at such times, we have witnessed emerging clarity and agency, and a greater sense of self-in-community, with a future. What we have seen to be true for individuals and groups of students could be true of this college and, indeed, all of academe.

Appendix

Methods

Using a mixed-methods approach, capitalizing on observations, community artifacts, and campus climate surveys, we tell a credible story of one institution's delimited awareness of sexual violence within its community. Relying on larger data sets, such as the Association of American Universities (AAU) surveys of universities (2017, 2020), we make the case that our story is representative.

The College

Our surveys, college artifacts, and local observations were limited to a small, private, coeducational liberal arts college in the Mid-Atlantic. Across our surveys (Spring semesters 2015–2022), the racial and gender compositions of the college were in flux, but on average 67.5 percent of the students identified as women and 58.8 percent identified as white. The self-reported gender and racial compositions are summarized in Table A1, as are the college's official tallies.

Campus Climate Surveys

Our surveying practice was kickstarted by a student research team in 2009, overseen by Rick at their request. Their survey was succinct, focusing on sexual assault prevalence and student awareness. Rick readministered their survey in 2012, with minor edits. The 2009 and 2012 surveys were not "campus climate" surveys per se; rather, they focused on the prevalence and awareness of sexual assault and gave some attention to situational factors, coercion, and consent ambiguities. Those early surveys, with participation

Table A1

Enrollment and participation by gender, race, and survey year

	Survey year				
	2015	2016	2018	2020	2022
Spring enrollments					
Total	1,389	1,419	1,347	1,393	989
Females/males	947/442	968/451	916/431	944/449	646/343
White/nonwhite	918/471	920/517	786/561	735/658	514/475
Participation: n (%)					
Completed parts I–II[a]	646 (47)	679 (48)	541 (40)	438 (31)	150 (15)
Completed full survey	610 (44)	639 (45)	473 (35)	389 (28)	132 (13)
Woman/man[b]	457/138	450/158	347/93	284/74	76/29
White/nonwhite	449/161	460/179	304/169	260/129	92/40

a. Through the demographic and climate questions, respectively, composing roughly 20% of the surveys.
b. The numbers of participants identifying as "nonbinary or other gender" were 15, 31, 33, 31, and 28, respectively.

rates of nearly 50 percent, established sexual assault prevalence, and student awareness thereof, commensurate with findings at other institutions. Working with teams of interested students and staff,[1] we redesigned the surveys in 2015 to comply with emergent federal recommendations that all institutions conduct regular campus climate surveys to monitor community safety and preparedness (e.g., U.S. Department of Education, Office for Civil Rights 2011a; White House Task Force to Protect Students from Sexual Assault 2014). Since 2016, state law has stipulated that climate surveys be administered biennially; consequently, we revised and administered climate surveys in the Spring semesters of 2015, 2016, 2018, 2020, and 2022, and beginning in 2016 we prepared and submitted mandated climate survey reports to the state.[2]

As shown in Table A1, participation rates were high across the first three campus climate surveys considered here and lower in 2020 and 2022, hovering near 50 percent in 2015 and 2016, near 40 percent in 2018, and falling to 31 and 14 percent, respectively, in 2020 and 2022. Survey procedures and incentives were held constant, so we are unsure why participation declined precipitously across the last two iterations. We suspect it was due largely to the COVID-19 pandemic, as students were sent home for remote instruction or temporary withdrawal in the middle of the 2020 survey and did not return "in residence" until just prior to the launch of the 2022 survey.

Table A2
Campus climate survey content timeline

	Content: Questions regarding:	Comments
2015 and subsequent surveys	Sexual assault, and context; demographics; campus climate; college responsiveness; reporting; telling; preparedness; sexual violence; awareness/attitudes regarding policies, Title IX, resources, consent, rape myths, etc. Open-ended follow-up questions.	Faculty, staff, and students designed/administered a campus climate survey in accordance with the White House Task Force to Protect Students from Sexual Assault
2016	Added: impact checklist; whom told; if received personal disclosures	Biennial surveys mandated by the state
2018	Added: impact scales; probes regarding "personal disclosures"	
2020	Added: probes regarding telling/ listening	COVID-19, remote instruction for nearly two years
2022	[*Replication of 2020 survey*]	Students returned to campus just prior to survey launch

Our various quantitative data summaries across the chapters are drawn from the 2015 through 2020 surveys. The qualitative data summaries and excerpts come from the 2015 survey forward, including 2022, as well as from other students' writings and testimonies. We also lean on our own experiences at the institution, before and during this period, as well as ongoing.

Survey Design

The surveys were designed and administered in accordance with the evolving needs of the college and the state and share many similarities and features of the survey guidelines developed during the Obama administration and conveyed on its "Not Alone" website. Though we revised and extended successive surveys responsively, none of our surveys were designed solely to test our ideas. Rather they were, first and foremost, campus climate surveys, and hence were principally designed to document, with replication, the college's adherence to federal and state guidelines. Our interest in the sexual assault awareness field grew over time, and we adjusted the surveys accordingly, but always at their margins. Our approach was to leverage the surveys, to the extent they allowed, to piece together a credible story of one institution's enduring, uneven, sexual assault awareness field.

In this way, secondary to documenting campus climate, and building slowly on Rose et al.'s (2009) foundational interest in student awareness, we examined how information about within-community sexual assault and violence moves through the college community, or fails to do so, and at what costs to the community. Across surveys, especially since 2016, we added items and sections that probed tellings and listenings and the costs/benefits borne by relational knowing, and we increasingly asked participants to share with us, in their own words, their experiences with telling and listening and knowing-with. Table A2 characterizes key survey changes over time.

Scales

Chapter 3 includes summary statistics and graphs depicting student attitudes and personal impacts, as measures by various Likert-type scales. Sample items composing each of the scales are listed in Tables A3 to A6, along with each scale's Cronbach's alpha, a measure of a scale's internal consistency.

Limitations

Our research design shares characteristics with the "case study," focused as it is on a single institution, bounded in time by our campus climate surveys running from 2015 to 2022, and drawing upon the data from students who

Table A3
Example items: College responsiveness

- I think staff (non-teaching) and administrators are genuinely concerned about my welfare.
- The faculty, staff and administrators at this school treat students fairly.
- College officials (administrators, campus safety officers) should do more to protect students from harm. [flipped]
- There are effective support systems on campus for students going through difficult times.

NOTE: The survey contained twelve 4-point disagree/agree Likert-type items. Cronbach's $\alpha = .841$.

Table A4
Example items: College's responsiveness to sexual assault complaints

The college would take:

... the report seriously
... corrective action to address factors that may have led to the sexual assault
... corrective action against the accused if found responsible for a violation of the policy
... steps to protect the person making the report from retaliation

NOTE: The survey contained eight 4-point unlikely/likely Likert-type items. Cronbach's $\alpha = .905$.

Table A5
Matched scales: College/university responsiveness to sexual assault or sexual misconduct complaints

AAU Survey Likely that campus officials would:	Our Surveys The college would: (college officials handle):
. . . . support students reporting	. . . take the report seriously
. . . protect safety of students reporting	. . . take steps to protect the safety of the person making the report
. . . conduct fair investigation	. . . incidents of misconduct relating to sexual and/or physical violence in a fair and responsible manner
. . . take action against offender	. . . take corrective action against the accused if found responsible for a violation of the policy
. . . address factors leading to sexual misconduct	. . . take corrective action to address factors that may have led to the sexual assault

NOTE: Cronbach's α = .892 (AAU), .883 (college).

Table A6
Example items: Impact scales

Activism

Empathy (Three Items)
- Greater empathy for survivors
- Greater understanding of the effects of sexual assault on others

Action (Two Items)
- Increased participation in programming or events that address sexual assault
- Greater involvement in activism around these issues

Academic (Seven Items)
- Missed class
- Grades dropped
- Trouble completing assignments

Psychological (Nine Items)
- Wanted to be alone
- Increased anxiety
- Felt numb or checked out

Social Behavioral (Eight Items)
- Engaged in more high-risk sexual activities
- Increased alcohol/drug use
- Withdrew from friends and/or activities

NOTE: 4-point "no change" to "major change" Likert-type items. Cronbach's α, per scale, = .906, .902, .914, .936, and .893, respectively.

elected to participate and upon archival materials, such as the student periodical *Hear My Voice*, Clery records, college missives and policies, and our own encounters and recollections.[3] In one sense then, ours is a "once-upon-a-time" story of a small, liberal arts, coeducational college blissfully attending to normative, day-to-day priorities. In that way, the emergent patterns we've identified—the story we tell—are irrevocably tied to the particulars of this college as it was during that period. The college continues to evolve demographically and fundamentally, to the point that it is not far-fetched to say that today's version is vastly different from the one we studied. Today the students who identify as white are the minority, to name one example; the faculty, staff, and administrators have likewise come and gone, and the academic program itself has been revamped (and continues to be). What use then is this story? Because we have focused on the landmark patterns within the school's epistemic field, rather than its micro-elements, and because we have demonstrated similar patterns exist at other, vastly different universities (AAU 2017, 2020), we are confident our findings represent an insidiousness, and indeed also a hopefulness, that can be found in most academic settings and indeed within most communities. There would exist a triadic epistemic field where survivors most often tell those they trust will hold the secret, and knowledges seep laterally by whisper among those who need to know. Invariably there will be avoiders, passive and active.

Acknowledgments

We appreciate the many students, faculty, and staff who inspired and supported our work over the years, especially the students who honored one another and us by telling, listening, carrying what they knew, as secrets, whispers, or shouts from the rooftops. Thank you for allowing us in. For those of you unable to tell, we hear you in your silence. This book is for all of you.

We thank the following for their direct support and involvement, devoting themselves to the project at critical times. To Jenna Rose, Leah Bailey, and Paige Kretschmar for seeing the need and getting it started; to Cynthia Terry, Roshelle Kades, Lucia Perfetti Clark, Sharon Spector, and Bill Leimbach for being there relationally as advocates and experts every step of the way; to Emily Collins, Ali Warhaftig, and Emma Cornell for your push, brilliance, and student research-team leadership in the early years; to Lily Reiser, Kalie Ganum, Susan Stocker, and Dena Smith for your thoughtful input; and to all of you who joined the team and advanced the work: Maggie Ratrie, Dana Ehrentreu, Soliana Goldrich, Jeremy Hardy, Joe Alston, Blake Flournoy, Ivelisse Rivera, Anna Bloomfield, Sarojini Schutt, Elaine Millas, and Eliza Owen-Smith. It was a pleasure. Thank you, all.

We are also appreciative of Peter Mickulus at Rutgers University Press for his encouragement and support throughout this process, and the helpful insights of our reviewers and editors.

JANET: I am grateful for the love and support of my family, whose sustained encouragement carried me across the finish line. To my husband, Dick, thank you for all you do, for picking up the tasks that freed me to work on this project in the evenings and on weekends. For my sons and daughter-in-law, may you know the wonder of having your work align with your life's passions. To Rick, thank you for sounding the siren about sexual violence for decades and for inviting me to collaborate with you. It has been a delight to think through these ideas with you.

RICK: Thank you, Janet, for this challenging, satisfying adventure, and for astonishing me when you said, "There's a book here." My thanks also to my daughters, sons-in law, and grandchildren who inspire my faith that a better world is within our reach. I am truly blessed by my life partner, touchstone, and friend, Cathy, without whose love and care my work on this project could not have happened. Thank you, my one, for all you do and for all you have done to make this possible.

Notes

Introduction

1   Most first-name attributions are pseudonyms. Occasionally, we altered identifying information to protect identities. Exceptions are when we quote our reminiscences, using "Janet" and "Rick," respectively.

2   Students' lived experiences figure prominently in our teaching and research praxis. Students may have confided in us accordingly.

3   Stories of an incident might emerge slowly. Listeners may help generate "resonance" to voice what might yet be said (e.g., Brown and Gilligan 1992; Gilligan 2023). Emergent stories might themselves be storied as in Kali's narrative in our book's opening. While a telling might not initially resemble a story, it minimally alludes to that possibility, serving as a placeholder and invitation for virtuous listeners to extend and join.

4   As quoted by Kingkade (2016). See also Banyard (2014).

5   We refer to students who have experienced sexual assault as survivors. We recognize not all would identify as survivors. Some may not process the experience in terms of survival (or even victimization). As Francisco (2000) points out, it is important to remember that not all victims of sexual violence survive the experience; some die. Additionally, students who do survive the experience may not survive as college students.

6   We understand telling is not for everyone. Many compelling reasons for silence exist.

7   The invitation need not be explicit. Compassionate attentiveness might be sufficient for the speakers to say what needs to be said, allowing them to stay in control and to navigate the relational complexities at play.

8   The distinction between "knowing that" and "knowing how" figures importantly in Western epistemology, or that branch of philosophy that deals with the nature of knowledge (e.g., Snowdon 2004; Stanley 2011). Alexis Shotwell (2017) argues for an expansive consideration of nonpropositional knowledges. We agree. We think of "relating to another," or knowing-with, as a rich epistemic resource, aspects of which run orthogonally to and complement the rational, truth-verifiable knowledge-that axis. Knowing-with incorporates all one's epistemic

resources, including the nonpropositional: the implicit perceptual, affective, and empathic capacities and features that are activated in connection with others. Much of what one knows about one's assault, pretelling, likely resides in the nonpropositional. Some of it might be *tacit*, which is to say, as Shotwell notes, that it is potentially, but perhaps not yet, known propositionally, or not yet sayable. One of the features of knowing-with, as we have come to understand it, is its capacity and inclination to avail the unsayable to be spoken and, hence, to be known in a different way and understood more fully.

9 As educators, we are reminded of the power of active learning, teaching strategies that privilege interactive, collaborative techniques, over pedagogies that emphasize passive listening and rote memorization. We are mindful of the importance of empathy and connection in how people learn and know (e.g., Belenky et al. 1986; Jordan 2017; Maureen Walker 2019; Melanie Walker 2019). On embodied ways of knowing, see Barbour (2004, 2018). For a review of feminist critiques of patriarchal conceptions of knowledge, see Mozeley and McPhillips (2019). Neuroscience, too, makes the case that emotion is essential in learning and knowing (e.g., Immordino-Yang 2015).

10 Polanyi (1958) argued that all knowing is at least partly tacit, involving aspects of knowing of which the person may be unaware and about which speech is not possible. We argue that knowing-with, in its dependence on perception, capacities to surmise and interpret affect in context and to empathize within the deeper aspects of what it means to be a friend is highly tacit and nonpropositional. There can certainly be a rational, Sherlockian approach to interpreting a situation, but some of what Medina (2013) refers to as "virtuous listening" runs more deeply than language and proposition, and important aspects reside in relationship.

11 The etymology of "tell" is complex. We acknowledge restricting, perhaps repurposing the word. Our usage links best to the Danish term, *tale*—speech, discourse, etc.

12 By active listener we mean the relationship and engagement are primary, and the conveyance, while important, is secondary to "being there" as a listener. Conveyance is enabled within the relationship and the active listening.

13 See Dick and Ziering (2016).

14 See the appendix for descriptions of our surveys and methodology.

15 We focus mostly on AAU's first survey because its questions more closely align with ours. Still, to the extent possible, we have examined their second survey, also, and in every instance the patterns discerned there replicate those we highlight in the chapters that follow.

Chapter 1 The Secret World of "Tellings"

1 These results replicate the pattern found in 2018.

2 Many institutional speech restrictions are inscribed in law, such as the Health Insurance Portability and Accountability Act (HIPAA) governing disclosures related to medical records (e.g., Colletti 2000) and the Family Educational Rights and Privacy Act (FERPA) governing privacy of students' educational records. These frameworks intersect and sometimes collide (e.g., Daggett 2020).

3 Rule violations can be costly. Rick recalls a student who chose to alert her friend's mom about her friend's self-destructive behavior knowing she would lose her friend.

4 "The talk" references other painful parent-to-child tellings, also, as when Black parents forewarn children about the perils of racism and white entitlement (e.g., Anderson et al. 2022; Douglas 2017).

5 Antioch College adopted an ongoing-verbal-consent policy in 1991. It was widely mocked (e.g., "'Ask First' at Antioch," *New York Times*, October 11, 1993, 16, and the *Saturday Night Live* skit "Is It Date Rape" that aired October 2, 1993). Samantha Stark (2018) provides a vindicating retrospective.

6 In the twentieth century, wives, girlfriends, and sex workers were not allowed to bring assault charges and women of color were not allowed to testify in courts (Alcoff 2018).

7 Carrying a fifty-pound mattress while on campus, in accordance with rules they generated, was Emma Sulkowicz's senior year performative art thesis, titled "Mattress Performance (Carry That Weight)," to signify what occurs in private, intimate spaces. Their project and case received national attention, as did a lawsuit filed by the accused against Columbia University. For an interview of Emma Sulkowicz at the time, see Smith (2014).

8 See her own article, "I Started the Media Men List," *The Cut*, January 10, 2018. The media response was critical of using this method as an extension of the whisper network used historically by women to warn women.

9 E.g., *The Hunting Ground* (Dick and Ziering 2016), which documents the preponderance of sexual assault on campuses, and Kantor and Twohey's (2020) *She Said*, which tells of the gathering of stories of harassment and assault perpetrated by Harvey Weinstein. See also *Know My Name*, Chanel Miller's (2020) first-person narrative of her experience following sexual assault by Brock Turner.

Chapter 2   The Uneven Relational-Knowledge Field

1 Jenna Rose, Paige Kretschmar, and Leah Bailey. We refer to them by their first names in the context of their time at the college as seniors—2008–2009.

2 See Rose et al. (2009).

3 "Sexual violence" is an umbrella term including sexual assault, sexual harassment, and interpersonal relationship violence. The climate survey asks about all three categories.

4 Some gaps reside beneath the field itself, rendering them unknowable within the field (Dotson 2014). These deeper gaps define implicitly what is not yet conceivable, what questions cannot yet be composed. For those, the available epistemic resources are inadequate.

5 Over 80 percent have experienced sexual violence defined more inclusively or know others within the community who have.

6 Remember, we are speaking of averages. Every person's experience is their own and need not adhere to an average.

7 We worked with the scale for over a year before we realized and acknowledged it did not rely on questions about formal knowledge and was tapping relational knowing, not procedural or propositional knowing.

Chapter 3   What One Needs to Know

1 Student survivors and their allies at the college occasionally self-published in-house essays, artwork, and poetry, titled *Hear My Voice*, for over a decade

(1995–2012). The title of the publication was a call to those in the community to listen, to take in their images and their words, and to begin to know with them. We withhold their names to protect confidentiality.

2 E.g., the AAU Reports (2017, 2020), and for a gateway reference for international findings and perspectives, see Chandrashekar et al. (2018).

3 For a variety of reasons related to the evolving composition of our surveys and to our increasing interest in the epistemic field, we widened our focus from knowledge of sexual assault within the community to knowledge of sexual violence within the community. This lessens the proportion of "not-knowers," since the category is more restricted, and enlarges the proportions of "know of others" and "survivors," since those categories are less restrictive. Importantly, the patterns we unveil are largely the same, and there remains the epistemic triad: sizable proportions of not-knowers, knowers, and survivors, in this case defining a relational knowledge of sexual violence scale. We are assuming, and our findings show, that these various ways of empirically defining the triadic knowing scale are all proxy to "relational knowing" or, in other words, indicators of student involvement in whisper networks.

4 Rick experienced this friction when attending his first Speak Out in 1991. Many female-presenting students, whom he knew personally, spoke of their experiences with sexual violence. He was shocked by the mismatch between his life and theirs. To the degree that social, epistemic frictions such as these afford opportunity for participants to connect with one another more deeply and realistically, their relatedness, their "we," can shift to the foreground—acknowledged and tended.

5 This kind of discomfort and avoidance can operate at the institutional level also.

6 They are more likely oblique to dominant narratives. This idea, that dominant narratives and frames are epistemically insular, has an expansive history. It undergirds Medina's (2013) argument but is also a central tenant within the fields of epistemic justice, feminist standpoint theory, critical race theory, and postcolonial critiques of logical/scientific positivism.

7 E.g., via climate surveys, Title IX offices, Clery reports, etc.

8 Our surveys were conducted early in the second semester. Hence, first-year students had half a year to acclimate to the community. Had the surveys been conducted earlier, the first-year proportion of avoiders would have certainly been higher.

9 All means are unweighted. The unweighted means best describe the community and its epistemic field, without adjustments for there being more women than men overall or more first-year students than seniors.

10 Alternative explanations for the lower proportions of avoiders among the upper classes are possible. For example, avoiders might be more likely than knowers and survivors to drop out or transfer. Perhaps upper-class avoiders are, for some reason, more likely to opt out of the survey. More research is needed to evaluate the possibilities. For now, we favor the simple one: that with time at the school, some avoiders come to know.

11 "Knowledge of sexual violence" is inclusive of answering "yes" to behaviorally defined queries about knowing of other students who have experienced sexual assault or intimate partner violence and/or emotional abuse since enrolling. Analyses that focus on the cost of knowing that others in the community have experienced sexual assault specifically reveal equivalent patterns as those shown here.

12 Perceived impact on the individual is also needed in some cases.

13 For further context, the vertical axis potentially ranges from −15 to +15, where 0.0 represents neither agreeing nor disagreeing, on average, within the group. Confidence Intervals (95 percent) are included for each bar in this and all subsequent figures.

14 Example survey items composing the scales referenced in this chapter are listed in the appendix.

15 The AAU's data are extensive, allowing for layered analyses involving subpopulations (see AAU 2017, 2020). We replicated our AAU analyses above (regarding how students viewed the university's likely responsiveness to a sexual misconduct complaint) separately for students who identified as white and for students who identified as nonwhite. The same patterns held.

16 Establishing that two variables are related, such as knowing someone in the community has been assaulted and having a positive regard for affirmative consent, does not necessarily mean one is driving the other. It simply establishes that these things tend to occur together. It might be, as one counterexample, that being "consent positive" is a feature of being receptive to "knowing-with" and for being a virtuous listener, especially when it comes to tellings about sexual violence, in which case the attitude would drive the knowing. Realistically, it likely goes both ways and many ways, with other variables entering the milieu, perhaps spiraling increasingly into awareness and relatedness, into situatedness within trusting social networks where whisperings are welcomed and heard. Still, it would seem that "coming into knowing," however one might get there, would contribute to what manifests thereafter in attitudes, beliefs, and actions.

17 Transformative learning is complex relationally and cognitively (e.g., Freire 1970; Mezirow 2003). Consider, for example, the challenges in forming a positive nonracist identity within a racist, white-supremacist culture (e.g., Helms 1990; Sue et al. 2015). These personal, epistemic transitions, however necessary, can be daunting, and the temptations to turn back often loom large.

18 We use "recovery" in the sense of Judith Herman's landmark book (1992), where it is understood to be uncertain, but holds the possibility of reconnection with the ordinariness of life.

19 The ratings in the left-hand panel exclude any within-scale items left unchecked or to which the student checked "no-change." Column heights reflect the average of the nonzero impact self-ratings within each scale, maximizing each scale's sensitivity.

20 Categorizing kinds of sexual violence as being "less" or "more" or "most" severe is presumptuous, we know, and any such attempts, including ours, should be regarded skeptically and critically. Everyone's experience is their own. We are referring only to averages, and for our data it is the case that those who situated their experiences as unwanted sexual contact, for example, reported fewer impacts on average than those who situated their experiences as unwanted, nonconsented, sexual penetration. While we acknowledge and mourn that sexual violence is commonplace and that its effects are often traumatic, we are more interested here in how simply knowing that it occurs and has occurred in one's local community can likewise carry heavy consequences and that the epistemic fault lines of knowing or not knowing are consequential for the community in ways invisible.

21 These findings are robust. We have looked at the data in multiple ways, and the results and conclusions have refused to go away. For example, if a personal impact

is redefined as existing only when the knower or survivor indicates there was a "major" change on one of the queried items, and then the number of those major changes indicated per scale is used as the dependent variable, the patterns still hold, graphically and statistically.

Chapter 4   The Secret Keepers

1   Bruner (2003, 17) describes a peripeteia as a sudden reversal in circumstances that turns a routine sequence of events into a breach in ordinariness.
2   Climate data from the Association of American Universities (2017, 2020) reveal a similar pattern: between 75 and 80 percent, depending on the nature of the assault, have told a friend about the incident.
3   We avoid referring to this as a "decision," which implies a level of intentionality that may or may not be present. An upset survivor could share the experience in response to a friend's probe, "What's wrong? What happened?" In response, words could pour out without conscious deliberation.
4   We refer to the assault as an experience to recognize that not all students have defined the incident as an assault (though all have met the behavioral definition of assault).
5   Though not the focus of this chapter, family members, therapists, and clergy may also function as secret keepers. Our data suggest a delay between the incident and these forms of telling. By the time they tell therapists and family members, survivors have begun to assign meaning to the experience and to define what has happened in a way that is recognizable to others. Society grants therapists and clergy the right to hold secrets via the confidentiality bestowed by their professions. A family member may agree to hold the secret or may opt to tell authorities.

Chapter 5   Say Nothing

1   There is an expansive research literature on embodied knowledge and wisdom, much of it springing from increasing understanding of individual- and community-level trauma, specifically, and of mental illness, community woundedness, and liberation epistemologies more generally. Here, we are thinking most specifically and historically of the landmark studies on *Women's Ways of Knowing* by Mary Belenky et al. (1986), *The Body Keeps Score: Brian, Mind, and Body in the Healing of Trauma* by Bessel van der Kolk (2014), and *Trauma and Recovery* and *Truth and Repair* by Judith Herman (2015, 2023). Note, also, the "unspeakable" knowledge held by many Holocaust survivors (e.g., Kidron 2009; Lentin 2000).
2   Entitlement sometimes manifests as over-the-top leniency, as in the Brock Turner case (e.g., Gersen 2023).
3   Some survivors may not be able to choose; they may have no words or capacity to formulate a subjectivity of the incident that would lend itself to telling. This is akin to what Belenky et al. (1986) referred to as "silence," one of the ways of knowing they discovered and considered in their landmark research. The capacity to tell, and also one's willingness to do so, even if just indirectly or in snippets initially, might well arise within the relational safety and encouragement of virtuous listening from a trustworthy friend. Journaling might help also (e.g., Pennebaker 2012).
4   A few institutions, like this one, require that consent be given verbally.

Chapter 6 Telling on Others

1 Examples of other notifications include reports to and from public safety officers, Clery notices issued by faculty and staff, climate survey reports, and direct disclosures from affected students—the latter considered hearsay until "properly" reported and adjudicated through Title IX.

2 At first glance, Clery reports might appear to be official in the sense that we mean, but they do not require college intervention. Also, they are not used reliably. When used, they are anonymous, abbreviated, individualized, categorized, tallied, and entered into yearly federal reports. In our experience, they grossly underestimate prevalence and are ignored at every level. Similarly, regarding students seeking help from campus health services, including counseling, while their stories are likely enabled with virtuous listening, the information is held in strict confidence. Of course, we understand why these safeguards are appropriate and necessary, but it is, nevertheless, another way the information is routed away from what the college knows officially.

3 One positive word that describes those who tell-on—"whistleblower"—is an exception, perhaps, and, not surprisingly, it is regulated in policies and statute, and it is a term better suited for naming individualized, institutional violations than for naming and conveying community harms (i.e., https://www.dol.gov/general/topics/whistleblower). Whistleblowers are often punished, and whistleblowing regulations, like the rules regulating Title IX, are in principle designed to offer some protection for coming forward, including various rules concerning whom, when, and how to tell, and they offer a degree of confidentiality, at least early in the process.

4 It's interesting to think of "telling-to" happening within the ever-present possibilities of telling-on, the latter being one of the escalations the silent holders likely want to avoid, and why the secret keepers whisper. Activating this epistemic automaton is not done lightly, and it can be triggered too easily, losing control. Mandatory reporters are likely nearby.

5 Not all assaults involve fellow students, and Title IX is not obligated to respond when the perpetrator is not a student and the incident occurs off campus.

6 The percentage of victims/survivors of sexual assault who sought help from on-campus counseling services is higher than for other campus services. One-quarter to one-third of survivors at the college reported they talked about their assault with a therapist or mental health professional.

7 Stone's (2020) research on faculty disclosures finds that even when faculty are aware of their role as mandatory reporters, only about a quarter follow through with the mandated report. Her findings suggest that the gap between faculty action and institutional mandate is not informational but rather a gap in confidence in the institutional management of sexual assault. The faculty in Stone's study report a greater sense of obligation to the student than to the institution.

8 The weight of a feather: In the case of sexual assaults, the Obama administration recognized the limits of adopting a stance of strong objectivity given the evidence available to weigh competing claims about sexual assault. Hence, federal guidelines established a preponderance of evidence standard, sometimes referred to as 50 percent and the weight of a feather, as the evidentiary standard. This standard, commonly applied in civil cases, means that if it is more likely than not the assault

occurred, the respondent will be found responsible. This standard requires less evidence than the clear and convincing standard, the higher standard of proof applied in criminal cases.

Clear and compelling: Under the 2020 regulations, colleges can choose whether to apply the preponderance of evidence or the clear and convincing standard to Title IX cases. However, the standard applied in Title IX cases must be the same standard applied to all employees, mirroring what is stipulated in collective bargaining agreements and faculty governance procedures (U.S. Department of Education, Office for Civil Rights 2021).

9 In a *New York Times* opinion piece, Bennett (2023) points out that "we don't ask victims of other violent crimes if they screamed out—to the contrary, *not* screaming is considered a way to not further provoke. Why, then, when it comes to victims of sexual violence, are those tropes so baked in?"

10 The Obama administration strongly discouraged cross-examinations due to the potential that cross-examination might be traumatic or intimidating to the survivor but stopped short of prohibiting them. The Trump administration tried to impose them, but they were overturned in a federal court case. The 2020 Title IX regulations have not eliminated cross-examinations as part of the process. However, they have tried to make them less traumatic, i.e., the survivor doesn't have to be in the same room as the respondent.

11 Keep in mind that 30.1 percent of the students participating in our surveys reported being sexually assaulted prior to enrolling in college, 13.7 percent of men and 37.5 percent of women and nonbinary.

12 According to the federal government, knowledge shared with campus authorities is referred to as actual or official knowledge. Knowledge that circulates among students isn't viewed as actual knowledge and, consequently, is considered unactionable.

13 Such as disclosures to health professionals or clergy, or stories told at campus "Speak Outs" and "Take Back the Night" rallies typically overseen by the college.

Conclusion

1 These include experience of sexual assault, campus climate, disclosure and reporting, knowledge of policies and resources, context of sexual assault, and other forms of violence.

2 It wasn't until we encountered notable works in social epistemology (e.g., Alcoff 2018; Bailey 2014; Dotson 2014; Fricker 2017; Medina 2013) that we were able to name this puzzle as an "epistemic injustice" arising directly from an uneven knowing field.

3 Survey evidence from the 1950s (Kanin 1957) documents sexual violence among college students, a finding replicated in Koss's (1985; Koss et al. 1987) groundbreaking research.

4 What initially started as a legislative nudge in the revision of Title IX in 2001 to recognize sexual violence became a legislative push when the Office of Civil Rights and the Department of Education under the Obama administration issued the 2011 Dear Colleague Letter (DCL) to respond to complaints that colleges and universities were not actively seeking this knowledge and responding to student complaints. In addition to reminding colleges and universities about their obligations under federal civil rights laws, the DCL mandated that colleges

designate a Title IX coordinator to respond to reports and offer survivors resources (Sharp et al. 2017). The DCL also provided guidelines about how schools should handle sexual violence through specific policies related to allegations and investigations. Drawing on this guidance, colleges and universities implemented or expanded their institutional structures and clarified their sexual misconduct policies and the processes for reporting an assault. As a result, offices with trained professionals tasked with carrying out institutional policies and procedures are now part of the epistemological field.

5   Medina (2013) describes this meta-blindness as an unawareness one has blind spots, a lack of awareness of one's susceptibility to ignorance. Meta-blindness is situated within the social imaginary; it delimits awareness, understanding, responsibility, and remedy.

6   As Alcoff (2018) reminds us, the metaphor of giving voice to sexual violence was pervasive throughout the early movement: survivor demonstrations were referred to as "Speak Outs."

7   E.g., Augusto Boal's *Theatre of the Oppressed* (1985). Alison Bailey (2014) considered what it might take to disrupt what Dotson (2014) referred to as third-order epistemic oppressions, which are those that reside beneath the epistemic field. She calls on "affective, creative, or other non-cognitive responses" or approaches (68) and reminds us, "Audre Lorde for example, treats poetry as a source of illumination. It is though poetry, she says, that 'we give name to those ideas which are—until the poem—nameless and formless, about to be birthed, but already felt'" (67).

8   Popular versions of the Rosa Parks story often exclude another important point: she was in the South investigating the sexual assault of Black women. The silence around her work on sexual violence is another cultural tell. See McGuire (2011) for a discussion.

9   Their report first appeared in the *New York Times* in October 2017.

10 The disjuncture between a friend or responder or researcher reflexively, naively thinking that a survivor can and should tell, on the one hand, and the survivor's reluctance or inability to do so, on the other, can be profound (e.g., Fine 1992).

11 This is an epistemological struggle, also. We are thinking of Paulo Freire's epistemological curiosity and insightfulness (1970). What constitutes evidence and knowledge, and who gets to decide? And when the knowledge and evidence are assembled, who gets to tell the larger, representative story, to whom? Will anyone listen? Will it matter? The three students who launched the surveys in 2009 faithfully reached for the master's tools—in this case, a quantitative survey—to dismantle the master's house (Lorde 2012). They were, after all, in the master's school learning the master's ways. But, alas, we know this story. We need new tools.

12 Using a restorative justice (RJ) framework, the Truth and Reconciliation Commission (TRC) nevertheless provided opportunities for the community to know more fully what Apartheid wrought. Some colleges and universities have implemented limited RJ alternatives (alongside Title IX options) for responding to sexual violence (Williamsen and Wessel 2023). We appreciate RJ's attentiveness to personal and collective stories of harm and its recognition that justice is relational. While RJ recognizes that personal harms harm the community too, it is reactive and does not address the epistemic structures that favor the status quo.

Appendix

1 Many staff, administrative officers, and students were directly involved in the early survey redesign, delivery, and analysis. Many more were directly involved with subsequent surveys. We salute them in our acknowledgments.

2 Maryland college and university reports are aggregated and summarized biennially and are publicly available. The college adopted a different survey instrument in 2023–2024, administered by the Higher Education Data Sharing Consortium (HEDS). While some of the campus climate content and general findings of that survey are consistent with ours, it did not probe what students know, let alone how they came to know and what came with it.

3 On case study methods, see Yin (2018).

References

Advocates for Youth. 2021. "The Cost of Reporting: Perpetrator Retaliation, Institutional Betrayal, and Student Survivor Pushout." *Know Your IX*. https://www.advocatesforyouth.org/wp-content/uploads/2024/06/Know-Your-IX-2021-Cost-of-Reporting.pdf.

Afifi, Tamara D., Andrea Joseph, and Desiree Aldeis. 2008. "Why Can't We Just Talk About It? An Observational Study of Parents' and Adolescents' Conversations About Sex." *Journal of Adolescent Research* 23 (6): 689–721. https://doi.org/10.1177/0743558408323841.

Afifi, Walid A., and Tamara D. Afifi. 2009. "Avoidance Among Adolescents in Conversations About Their Parents' Relationship: Applying the Theory of Motivated Information Management." *Journal of Social and Personal Relationships* 26 (4): 488–511. https://doi.org/10.1177/0265407509350869.

Alcoff, Linda, and Laura Gray. 1993. "Survivor Discourse: Transgression or Recuperation?" *Signs: Journal of Women in Culture and Society* 18 (2): 260–290.

Alcoff, Linda Martín. 2018. *Rape and Resistance*. John Wiley.

Anderson, Elizabeth. 2012. "Epistemic Justice as a Virtue of Social Institutions." *Social Epistemology* 26 (2): 163–173. https://doi.org/10.1080/02691728.2011.652211.

Anderson, Leslie A., Margaret O'Brien Caughy, and Margaret T. Owen. 2022. "'The Talk' and Parenting While Black in America: Centering Race, Resistance, and Refuge." *Journal of Black Psychology* 48 (3–4): 475–506.

Anderson, Luvell. 2017. "Epistemic Injustice and the Philosophy of Race." In *The Routledge Handbook of Epistemic Injustice*, edited by Ian James Kidd, José Medina, and Gaile Pohlhaus, 139–148. Routledge.

Applebaum, Barbara. 2015. "Needing Not to Know: Ignorance, Innocence, Denials, and Discourse." *Philosophy of Education* 71:448–456. https://doi.org/10.47925/2015.448.

Association of American Universities. 2017. "Campus Climate Survey on Sexual Assault and Sexual Misconduct, 2010–2015." Inter-university Consortium for Political and Social Research. https://doi.org/10.3886/ICPSR36696.v1.

———. 2020. "Campus Climate Survey on Sexual Assault and Sexual Misconduct, 2014–2019." Inter-university Consortium for Political and Social Research. https://doi.org/10.3886/ICPSR37662.v1.

Bailey, Alison. 2014. "The Unlevel Knowing Field: An Engagement with Dotson's Third-Order Epistemic Oppression." *Social Epistemology Review and Reply Collective* 3 (10): 62–68.

Banham, Gary. 2012. "Kantian Friendship." In *Critical Communities and Aesthetic Practices*, edited by Francis Halsall, Julia Jansen, and Sinead Murphy, 171–180. Springer.

Banyard, Victoria L. 2014. "Improving College Campus–Based Prevention of Violence Against Women: A Strategic Plan for Research Built on Multipronged Practices and Policies." *Trauma, Violence, & Abuse* 15 (4): 339–351. https://doi.org/10.1177/1524838014521027.

Banyard, Victoria. L., Mary M. Moynihan, Wendy A. Walsh, Ellen S. Cohn, and Sally Ward. 2010. "Friends of Survivors: The Community Impact of Unwanted Sexual Experiences." *Journal of Interpersonal Violence* 25 (2): 242–256.

Barbour, Karen. 2004. "Embodied Ways of Knowing." *Waikato Journal of Education* 10:227–238.

———. 2018. "Embodied Ways of Knowing: Revisiting Feminist Epistemology." In *The Palgrave Handbook of Feminism and Sport, Leisure and Physical Education*, edited by Louise Mansfield, Jayne Caudwell, Belinda Wheaton, and Beccy Watson, 209–226. Palgrave.

Barker, Simon, Charlie Crerar, and Trystan S. Goetze. 2018. "Harms and Wrongs in Epistemic Practice." *Royal Institute of Philosophy Supplement* 84 (November): 1–21. https://doi.org/10.1017/S1358246118000528.

Bay-Cheng, Laina Y., and Rebecca K. Eliseo-Arras. 2008. "The Making of Unwanted Sex: Gendered and Neoliberal Norms in College Women's Unwanted Sexual Experiences." *Journal of Sex Research* 45 (4): 386–397. https://doi.org/10.1080/00224490802398381.

Bay-Cheng, Laina Y., Adjoa D. Robinson, and Alyssa N. Zucker. 2009. "Behavioral and Relational Contexts of Adolescent Desire, Wanting, and Pleasure: Undergraduate Women's Retrospective Accounts." *Journal of Sex Research* 46 (6): 511–524. https://doi.org/10.1080/00224490902867871.

Belenky, Mary Field, Blythe McVicker Clinchy, Nancy Rule Goldberger, and Jill Mattuck Tamle. 1986. *Women's Ways of Knowing: The Development of Self, Voice, and Mind*. Basic Books.

Bellman, Beryl L. 1981. "The paradox of secrecy." *Human Studies* 4 (1): 1–24.

Bennett, Jessica. 2023. "Why She Didn't Scream? And Other Questions Not to Ask a Rape Survivor." *New York Times*, May 2. https://www.nytimes.com/2023/05/01/opinion/e-jean-carroll-trial.html.

Bennett, Sidney, and Victoria L. Banyard. 2016. "Do Friends Really Help Friends? The Effect of Relational Factors and Perceived Severity on Bystander Perception of Sexual Violence." *Psychology of Violence* 6 (1): 64–72.

Boal, Augusto. 1985. *Theatre of the Oppressed*. Theatre Communications Group.

Brison, Susan J. 2002. *Aftermath: Violence and the Remaking of Self*. Princeton University Press.

Brown, Lyn Mikel, and Carol Gilligan. 1992. *Meeting at the Crossroads: Women's Psychology and Girls' Development*. Harvard University Press.

Bruner, Jerome Seymour. 2003. *Making Stories: Law, Literature, Life*. Harvard University Press.

Burnett, Ann, Jody L. Mattern, Liliana L. Herakova, David H. Kahl, Cloy Tobola, and Susan E. Bornsen. 2009. "Communicating/Muting Date Rape:

A Co-Cultural Theoretical Analysis of Communication Factors Related to Rape Culture on a College Campus." *Journal of Applied Communication Research* 37 (4): 465–485. https://doi.org/10.1080/00909880903233150.

Byron, Paul, and Jessie Hunt. 2017. "'That Happened to Me Too': Young People's Informal Knowledge of Diverse Genders and Sexualities." *Sex Education* 17 (3): 319–332. https://doi.org/10.1080/14681811.2017.1292899.

Cantor, David, Bonnie Fisher, Susan Chibnall, Shauna Harps, Reanne Townsend, Gail Thomas, Hyunshik Lee, Vanessa Kranz, Randy Herbison, and Kristin Madden. 2020. "Report on the AAU Campus Climate Survey on Sexual Assault and Misconduct." Association of American Universities, January 17. https://www.aau .edu/sites/default/files/AAU-Files/Key-Issues/Campus-Safety/Revised%20Aggre gate%20report%20%20and%20appendices%201-7_(01-16-2020_FINAL).pdf.

Cantor, David, Bonnie Fisher, Susan Chibnall, Reanne Townsend, Hyunshik Lee, Carol Bruce, and Gail Thomas. 2017. "Report on the AAU Campus Climate Survey on Sexual Assault and Misconduct." Association of American Universities, October 20. https://www.aau.edu/sites/default/files/AAU-Files/Key-Issues /Campus-Safety/AAU-Campus-Climate-Survey-FINAL-10-20-17.pdf.

Caron, Sandra L., and Deborah Mitchell. 2022. "'I've Never Told Anyone': A Qualitative Analysis of Interviews with College Women Who Experienced Sexual Assault and Remained Silent." *Violence Against Women* 28 (9): 1987–2009. https://doi.org /10.1177/10778012211022766.

Carter, J. Adam. 2020. "Trust and Its Significance in Social Epistemology." In *Oxford Handbook of Social Epistemology*, edited by Jennifer Lackey and Aidan McGlynn, 182–200. Oxford University Press.

Caughlin, John P., and Anita L. Vangelisti. 2015. "Why People Conceal or Reveal Secrets: A Multiple Goals Theory Perspective." In *Uncertainty, Information Management, and Disclosure Decisions,* edited by Tamara D. Afifi and Walid A. Afifi, 279–299. Routledge.

Chandrashekar, Karuna, Kimberly Lacroix, and Sabah Siddiqui. 2018. "Sex and Power in the University." *Annual Review of Critical Psychology* 15:3–14.

Chocano, Carina. 2020. "Savage Truths." *New York Times Magazine,* December 20, 44.

Coady, David. 2017. "Epistemic Injustice as Distributive Injustice 1." In *The Routledge Handbook of Epistemic Injustice,* edited by Ian James Kidd, José Medina, and Gaile Pohlhaus, 61–68. Routledge.

Code, Lorraine. 2008. "Advocacy, Negotiation, and the Politics of Unknowing." *Southern Journal of Philosophy* 46 (S1): 32–51. https://doi.org/10.1111/j.2041-6962 .2008.tb00152.x.

———. 2014. "Feminist Epistemology and the Politics of Knowledge: Questions of Marginality." *The SAGE Handbook of Feminist Theory,* edited by Mary Evans, Clare Hemmings, Marsha Henry, Hazel Johnstone, Sumi Madhok, Ania Plomien, and Sadie Wearing, 9–15. SAGE.

———. 2017. "Epistemic Responsibility." In *The Routledge Handbook of Epistemic Injustice,* edited by Ian James Kidd, José Medina, and Gaile Pohlhaus, 89–99. Routledge.

———. 2020. *Epistemic Responsibility.* State University of New York Press.

Colletti, Anthony C. 2000. "HIPAA: An Overview." *Health Law* 13:14.

Corbin, Elwood. 2021. *Too Scared to Tell: The Dark Side of Telling the Truth.* Design.

Cowan, Sarah K. 2020. "Secrets and Social Networks." *Current Opinion in Psychology* 31:99–104.

Crisp, Roger. 2014. *Aristotle: Nicomachean Ethics*. Cambridge University Press.

Daggett, Lynn M. 2020. "Female Student Patient 'Privacy' at Campus Health Clinics: Realities and Consequences." *University of Baltimore Law Review* 50: 77–153.

Daukas, Nancy. 2020. "Epistemic Justice and Injustice." In *The Routledge Handbook of Social Epistemology,* edited by Miranda Fricker, Peter J. Graham, David Henderson, and Nikolaj J.L.L. Pedersen, 327–334. Routledge.

DeLaet, Debra L., and Elizabeth Mills. 2018. "Discursive Silence as a Global Response to Sexual Violence: From Title IX to Truth Commissions." *Global Society* 32 (4): 496–519.

Dick, Kirby, and Amy Ziering. 2016. *The Hunting Ground: The Inside Story of Sexual Assault on American College Campuses*. Simon & Schuster.

Dieleman, Susan. 2012. "An Interview with Miranda Fricker." *Social Epistemology* 26 (2): 253–261. https://doi.org/10.1080/02691728.2011.652216.

Donegan, Moira. 2018. "I Started the Media Men List." *The Cut*, January 10. https://www.thecut.com/2018/01/moira-donegan-i-started-the-media-men-list.html.

———. 2021. "Another Reckoning over Sexual Assault in US Colleges Is Starting. Officials Must Listen." *The Guardian*, October 31. https://www.theguardian.com/commentisfree/2021/oct/31/sexual-assault-us-colleges-officials-must-listen.

Dormandy, Katherine. 2020. "Intellectual Humility and Epistemic Trust." In *The Routledge Handbook of Philosophy of Humility*, edited by Mark Alfano, Michael P. Lynch, and Alessandra Tanesini, 292–302. Routledge.

Dotson, Kristie. 2011. "Tracking Epistemic Violence, Tracking Practices of Silencing." *Hypatia* 26 (2): 236–257.

———. 2014. "Conceptualizing Epistemic Oppression." *Social Epistemology* 28 (2): 115–138. https://doi.org/10.1080/02691728.2013.782585.

———. 2015. "Inheriting Patricia Hill Collins's Black Feminist Epistemology." *Ethnic and Racial Studies* 38 (13): 2322–2328.

Douglas, Kelly Brown. 2017. "The Race of It All: Conversations Between a Mother and Her Son." In *Parenting as Spiritual Practice and Source for Theology: Mothering Matters*, edited by Claire Bischoff, Elizabeth O'Donnell Gandolfo, and Annie Hardison-Moody, 23–39. Palgrave Macmillan.

Dworkin, Emily R., Samantha L. Pittenger, and Nicole E. Allen. 2016. "Disclosing Sexual Assault Within Social Networks: A Mixed-Method Investigation." *American Journal of Community Psychology* 57 (1–2): 216–228.

Fallowfield, Lesley. 1993. "Giving Sad and Bad News." *Lancet* 341 (8843): 476–478.

Featherstone, Lisa, Cassandra Byrnes, Jenny Maturi, Kiara Minto, Renée Mickelburgh, and Paige Donaghy. 2024. *The Limits of Consent: Sexual Assault and Affirmative Consent*. Springer Nature.

Fine, Michelle. 1992. "Coping with Rape: Critical Perspectives on Consciousness." In *Disruptive Voices: The Possibilities of Feminist Research*, edited by Michelle Fine, 61–76. University of Michigan Press.

Foucault, Michel. 1977. *Discipline and Punish: The Birth of the Prison*. 1st Vintage ed. Vintage Books.

———. 1980. *Power/Knowledge: Selected Interviews and Other Writings 1972–1977*. Edited by Colin Gordan. New York: Pantheon

———. 2019. *The History of Sexuality: The Will to Knowledge*. Penguin.

Francis, Laura, and Noelle Robertson. 2023. "Healthcare Practitioners' Experiences of Breaking Bad News: A Critical Interpretative Meta Synthesis." *Patient Education and Counseling* 107:107574.

Francisco, Patricia Weaver. 2000. *Telling: A Memoir of Rape and Recovery.* HarperCollins.

Freire, Paulo. 1970. *Pedagogy of the Oppressed.* Continuum.

Freitas, Donna. 2013. *The End of Sex: How Hookup Culture Is Leaving a Generation Unhappy, Sexually Unfulfilled, and Confused About Intimacy.* Basic Books.

Fricker, Miranda. 2007. *Epistemic Injustice: Power and the Ethics of Knowing.* Oxford University Press.

———. 2013. "Epistemic Justice as a Condition of Political Freedom?" *Synthese* 190 (7): 1317–1332. https://doi.org/10.1007/s11229-012-0227-3.

———. 2017. "Evolving Concepts of Epistemic Injustice." In *The Routledge Handbook of Epistemic Injustice,* edited by Ian James Kidd, José Medina, and Gaile Pohlhaus, 53–60. Routledge.

Germain, Lauren J. 2016. *Campus Sexual Assault: College Women Respond.* Johns Hopkins University Press.

Gersen, Jeannie Suk. 2023. "Revisiting the Brock Turner Case." *New Yorker,* March 29. https://www.newyorker.com/news/our-columnists/revisiting-the-brock-turner-case.

Gilligan, Carol. 2023. *In a Human Voice.* John Wiley.

Goffman, Erving. 1963. *Stigma: Notes on the Management of Spoiled Identity.* Prentice Hall.

———. 1983. *Interaction Ritual.* Pantheon.

Goldfarb, Anna. 2020. "Reaching Out to Someone Who Is Having a Difficult Time." *New York Times,* July 27, B6.

Grasswick, Heidi E. 2010. "Scientific and Lay Communities: Earning Epistemic Trust Through Knowledge Sharing." *Synthese* 177 (3): 387–409. https://doi.org/10.1007/s11229-010-9789-0.

———. 2017. "Trust and Testimony in Feminist Epistemology." In *The Routledge Companion to Feminist Philosophy,* edited by Ann Garry, Serene J. Khader, and Alison Stone, 256–267. Routledge.

———. 2018. "Understanding Epistemic Trust Injustices and Their Harms." *Royal Institute of Philosophy Supplement* 84 (November): 69–91. https://doi.org/10.1017/S1358246118000553.

———. 2021. "Individuals-in-Communities: The Search for a Feminist Model of Epistemic Subjects." *Hypatia* 19 (3): 85–102.

Guerrero, Laura K., and Walid A. Afifi. 1995. "Some Things Are Better Left Unsaid: Topic Avoidance in Family Relationships." *Communication Quarterly* 43 (3): 276–296. https://doi.org/10.1080/01463379509369977.

Hall, Roberta M., and Bernice R. Sandler. 1982. "The Classroom Climate: A Chilly One for Women?" https://eric.ed.gov/?id=ED215628.

Hawley, Katherine. 2017. "Trust, Distrust, and Epistemic Injustice." In *The Routledge Handbook of Epistemic Injustice,* edited by Ian James Kidd, José Medina, and Gaile Pohlhaus, 69–78. Routledge.

Helms, Janet E. 1990. *Black and White Racial Identity: Theory, Research, and Practice.* Greenwood.

Herman, Judith L. 1992. *Trauma and Recovery: The Aftermath of Violence—From Domestic Abuse to Political Terror.* Basic Books.

———. 2015. *Trauma and Recovery: The Aftermath of Violence—From Domestic Abuse to Political Terror*. Hachette.

———. 2023. *Truth and Repair: How Trauma Survivors Envision Justice*. Hachette.

Hirsch, Jennifer S., and Shamus Khan. 2020. *Sexual Citizens: A Landmark Study of Sex, Power, and Assault on Campus*. Norton.

Immordino-Yang, Mary Helen. 2015. *Emotions, Learning, and the Brain: Exploring the Educational Implications of Affective Neuroscience*. Norton.

Jaschik, Scott, and Doug Lederman. 2015. "The 2015 Inside Higher Ed Survey of College and University Presidents." *Inside Higher Ed.* https://www.insidehighered .com/sites/default/files/media/2015%20IHE_PresidentsSurvey.pdf.

Jessup-Anger, Jody, Elise Lopez, and Mary P. Koss. 2018. "History of Sexual Violence in Higher Education: History of Sexual Violence in Higher Education." *New Directions for Student Services* 2018 (161): 9–19. https://doi.org/10.1002/ss.20249.

Jordan, Carol E. 2014. "The Safety of Women on College Campuses: Implications of Evolving Paradigms in Postsecondary Education." *Trauma, Violence, & Abuse* 15 (3): 143–148. https://doi.org/10.1177/1524838014520635.

Jordan, Judith V. 2017. "Relational-cultural Theory: The Power of Connection to Transform Our Lives." *Journal of Humanistic Counseling* 56 (3): 228–243.

Joseph, Andrea L, and Tamara D. Afifi. 2010. "Military Wives' Stressful Disclosures to Their Deployed Husbands: The Role of Protective Buffering." *Journal of Applied Communication Research* 38 (4): 412–434.

Jozkowski, Kristen N., Zoë D. Peterson, Stephanie A. Sanders, Barbara Dennis, and Michael Reece. 2014. "Gender Differences in Heterosexual College Students' Conceptualizations and Indicators of Sexual Consent: Implications for Contemporary Sexual Assault Prevention Education." *Journal of Sex Research* 51 (8): 904–916. https://doi.org/10.1080/00224499.2013.792326.

Kanin, Eugene J. 1957. "Male Aggression in Dating-Courtship Relations." *American Journal of Sociology* 63 (2): 197–204.

Kant, Immanuel. 2017. *Kant: The Metaphysics of Morals*. Cambridge University Press.

Kantor, Jodi, and Megan Twohey. 2017. "Harvey Weinstein Paid Off Sexual Harassment Accusers for Decades." *New York Times*, October 5. https://www.nytimes .com/2017/10/05/us/harvey-weinstein-harassment-allegations.html.

———. 2020. *She Said: Breaking the Sexual Harassment Story That Helped Ignite a Movement*. Bloomsbury.

Karjane, Heather M. 2005. "Sexual Assault on Campus: What Colleges and Universities Are Doing About It." U.S. Department of Justice, Office of Justice Programs, National Institute of Justice.

Kawall, Jason. 2013. "Friendship and Epistemic Norms." *Philosophical Studies* 165 (2): 349–370. https://doi.org/10.1007/s11098-012-9953-0.

Khan, Shamus R., Jennifer S. Hirsch, Alexander Wambold, and Claude A. Mellins. 2018. "'I Didn't Want To Be "That Girl"': The Social Risks of Labeling, Telling, and Reporting Sexual Assault." *Sociological Science* 5:432–460.

Kidron, Carol A. 2009. "Toward an Ethnography of Silence: The Lived Presence of the Past in the Everyday Life of Holocaust Trauma Survivors and Their Descendants in Israel." *Current Anthropology* 50:5–27.

Kingkade, Tyler. 2016. "There's No More Denying Campus Rape Is a Problem. This Study Proves It." *Huffington Post*, January 20, 2016; updated February 2, 2017. https://www.huffpost.com/entry/college-sexual-assault-study_n_569e928be4b0 cd99679b9ada.

Kirkner, Anne, Katherine Lorenz, Sarah E. Ullman, and Rupashree Mandala. 2018. "A Qualitative Study of Sexual Assault Disclosure Impact and Help-Seeking on Support Providers." *Violence and Victims* 33 (4): 721–738.

Klein, Renate. 2018. "Sexual Violence on US College Campuses: History and Challenges." In *Gender Based Violence in University Communities: Policy, Prevention and Educational Initiatives*, edited by Sundari Anitha and Ruth Lewis, 63–82. Policy Press.

Koss, Mary P. 1985. "The Hidden Rape Victim: Personality, Attitudinal, and Situational Characteristics." *Psychology of Women Quarterly* 9 (2): 193–212.

Koss, Mary P., Christine A. Gidycz, and Nadine Wisniewski. 1987. "The Scope of Rape: Incidence and Prevalence of Sexual Aggression and Victimization in a National Sample of Higher Education Students." *Journal of Consulting and Clinical Psychology* 55 (2): 162–170.

Koss, Mary P., Jay K. Wilgus, and Kaaren M. Williamsen. 2014. "Campus Sexual Misconduct: Restorative Justice Approaches to Enhance Compliance with Title IX Guidance." *Trauma, Violence, & Abuse* 15 (3): 242–257. https://doi.org/10.1177/1524838014521500.

Krause, Kathleen H., Rebecca Woofter, Regine Haardörfer, Michael Windle, Jessica M. Sales, and Kathryn M. Yount. 2019. "Measuring Campus Sexual Assault and Culture: A Systematic Review of Campus Climate Surveys." *Psychology of Violence* 9 (6): 611–622. https://doi.org/10.1037/vio0000209.

Krebs, Christopher P., Christine Lindquist, and Tara Warner. 2007. "The Campus Sexual Assault (CSA) Study." Inter-university Consortium for Political and Social Research, University of Michigan.

Lentin, Ronit. 2000. "Expected to Live: Women Shoah 1 Survivors' Testimonials of Silence." *Women's Studies International Forum* 23 (6): 689–700. https://doi.org/10.1016/S0277-5395(00)00141-2.

Lewis, Leslie W. 2007. *Telling Narratives: Secrets in African American Literature*. University of Illinois Press.

Liberman, Zoe. 2020. "Keep the Cat in the Bag: Children Understand That Telling a Friend's Secret Can Harm the Friendship." *Developmental Psychology* 56 (7): 1290–1304.

Linder, Chris, Niah Grimes, Brittany M. Williams, and Marvette C. Lacy. 2020. "What Do We Know About Campus Sexual Violence? A Content Analysis of 10 Years of Research." *Review of Higher Education* 43 (4): 1017–1040.

Logan, T. K., Robert Walker, and Jennifer Cole. 2015. "Silenced Suffering: The Need for a Better Understanding of Partner Sexual Violence." *Trauma, Violence, & Abuse* 16 (2): 111–135. https://doi.org/10.1177/1524838013517560.

Lorde, Audre. 2012. *Sister Outsider: Essays and Speeches*. Crossing Press.

Lui, Yuanyuan, Marilyn A. Campbell, and Chrystal Whiteford. 2022. "'Snitches Get Stitches': Why Most Bullied Young People Don't Disclose Incidents of Bullying and Harassment." In *Handbook of Racism, Xenophobia, and Populism: All Forms of Discrimination in the United States and Around the Globe*, edited by Adebowale Akande, 785–803. Springer.

Mann, Judy. 1990. "The Statistic No One Can Bear to Believe." *Washington Post*, December 5, D3.

Markle, Megan, the Duchess of Sussex. 2020. "The Losses We Share." *New York Times*, November 25, A23.

Martin, Sandra L., Bonnie S. Fisher, Tara D. Warner, Christopher P. Krebs, and Christine H. Lindquist. 2011. "Women's Sexual Orientations and Their

Experiences of Sexual Assault Before and During University." *Women's Health Issues* 21 (3): 199–205. https://doi.org/10.1016/j.whi.2010.12.002.

Mason, Cathy. 2021. "The Epistemic Demands of Friendship: Friendship as Inherently Knowledge-Involving." *Synthese* 199 (1–2): 2439–2455. https://doi.org/10.1007/s11229-020-02892-w.

McGuire, Danielle L. 2011. *At the Dark End of the Street: Black Women, Rape, and Resistance—A New History of the Civil Rights Movement from Rosa Parks to the Rise of Black Power*. Vintage.

McHugh, Nancy Arden. 2017. "Epistemic Communities and Institutions." In *The Routledge Handbook of Epistemic Injustice*, edited by Ian James Kidd, José Medina, and Gaile Pohlhaus, 270–278. Routledge.

Medina, José. 2013. *The Epistemology of Resistance: Gender and Racial Oppression, Epistemic Injustice, and Resistant Imaginations*. Oxford University Press.

———. 2017. "Varieties of Hermeneutical Injustice 1." In *The Routledge Handbook of Epistemic Injustice*, edited by Ian James Kidd, José Medina, and Gaile Pohlhaus, 41–52. Routledge.

———. 2018. "Misrecognition and Epistemic Injustice." *Feminist Philosophy Quarterly* 4 (4). https://doi.org/10.5206/fpq/2018.4.6233.

Mellins, Claude A., Kate Walsh, Aaron L. Sarvet, Melanie Wall, Louisa Gilbert, John S. Santelli, Martie Thompson, Patrick A. Wilson, Shamus Khan, and Stephanie Benson. 2017. "Sexual Assault Incidents Among College Undergraduates: Prevalence and Factors Associated with Risk." *PLOS One* 12 (11): e0186471.

Mezirow, Jack. 2003. "Transformative Learning as Discourse." *Journal of Transformative Education* 1:58–63.

Miller, Chanel. 2020. *Know My Name: A Memoir*. Penguin.

Misch, Antonia, Harriet Over, and Malinda Carpenter. 2016. "I Won't Tell: Young Children Show Loyalty to Their Group by Keeping Group Secrets." *Journal of Experimental Child Psychology* 142:96–106.

Mozeley, Fee, and Kathleen McPhillips. 2019. "Knowing Otherwise: Restorying Intuitive Knowing as Feminist Resistance." *Women's Studies* 48 (8): 844–861.

Mullaney, Jamie L. 2006. *Everyone Is NOT Doing It: Abstinence and Personal Identity*. University of Chicago Press.

O'Callaghan, Erin, Katherine Lorenz, Sarah E. Ullman, and Anne Kirkner. 2021. "A Dyadic Study of Impacts of Sexual Assault Disclosure on Survivors' Informal Support Relationships." *Journal of Interpersonal Violence* 36 (9–10): NP5033–59. https://doi.org/10.1177/0886260518795506.

O'Callaghan, Erin, and Sarah E. Ullman. 2022. "Exploring Correlates of Social Reactions to Disclosure Among Latina Sexual Assault Survivors." *Violence and Victims*. https://doi.org/10.1891/VV-2021-0015.

Orenstein, Peggy. 2024. "The Troubling Trend in Teenage Sex." *New York Times*, April 12. https://www.nytimes.com/2024/04/12/opinion/choking-teen-sex-brain-damage.html.

Patel, Vimal. 2023. "How a Yale Student's Rape Accusation Exposed Her to a Defamation Lawsuit." *New York Times*, September 17. https://www.nytimes.com/2023/09/17/us/yale-rape-case-defamation.html.

Pennebaker, James W. 2012. *Opening Up: The Healing Power of Expressing Emotions*. Guilford.

Pesch, Annelise, Sarah Suárez, and Melissa A. Koenig. 2018. "Trusting Others: Shared Reality in Testimonial Learning." *Current Opinion in Psychology* 23 (October): 38–41. https://doi.org/10.1016/j.copsyc.2017.11.009.

Piccigallo, Jacqueline R., Terry G. Lilley, and Susan L. Miller. 2012. "'It's Cool to Care About Sexual Violence': Men's Experiences with Sexual Assault Prevention." *Men and Masculinities* 15 (5): 507–525. https://doi.org/10.1177/1097184X12458590.

Pohlhaus, Gaile. 2012. "Relational Knowing and Epistemic Injustice: Toward a Theory of Willful Hermeneutical Ignorance." *Hypatia* 27 (4): 715–735. https://doi.org/10.1111/j.1527-2001.2011.01222.x.

———. 2017. "Varieties of Epistemic Injustice 1." In *The Routledge Handbook of Epistemic Injustice*, edited by Ian James Kidd, José Medina, and Gaile Pohlhaus, 13–26. Routledge.

Polanyi, Michael. 1958. *Personal Knowledge: Towards a Post-Critical Philosophy*. University of Chicago Press.

Proctor, Robert N., and Londa Schiebinger. 2008. *Agnotology: The Making and Unmaking of Ignorance*. Stanford University Press.

Redlick, Madeleine. 2017. "The Perceived Threat of Sexual Communication, Number of Previous Sexual Partners and Topic Avoidance in Romantic Relationships." *Psychology & Sexuality* 8 (1–2): 148–157. https://doi.org/10.1080/19419899.2017.1316768.

Roeder, Tara. 2015. "'You Have to Confess': Rape and the Politics of Storytelling." *Journal of Feminist Scholarship* 9 (9): 18–29.

Rose, Jenna, Paige Kretschmar, and Leah Bailey. 2009. "The Prevalence of Sexual Assault at [College]." Unpublished senior project.

Rothman, Karen, Emily Georgia Salivar, McKenzie K. Roddy, S. Gabe Hatch, and Brian D. Doss. 2021. "Sexual Assault Among Women in College: Immediate and Long-Term Associations with Mental Health, Psychosocial Functioning, and Romantic Relationships." *Journal of Interpersonal Violence* 36 (19–20): 9600–9622. https://doi.org/10.1177/0886260519870.

Ryan, Dan. 2006. "Getting the Word Out: Notes on the Social Organization of Notification." *Sociological Theory* 24 (3): 228–254. https://doi.org/10.1111/j.1467-9558.2006.00289.x.

Sandoz, Emily, and Louisiana Contextual Science Research Group. 2021. "Beyond 'Yes Means Yes': A Behavioral Conceptualization of Affirmative Sexual Consent." *Behavior and Social Issues* 30 (1): 712–731.

Sears-Greer, Mackenzie A., Bridget K. Friehart, and Cindy M. Meston. 2022. "A Review of Undergraduate Student Disclosures of Sexual Violence." *Sexual Medicine Reviews* 10 (4): 543–553. https://doi.org/10.1016/j.sxmr.2022.06.006.

Sharp, Elizabeth A., Shannon E. Weaver, and Anisa Zvonkovic. 2017. "Introduction to the Special Issue: Feminist Framings of Sexual Violence on College Campuses." *Family Relations* 66:7–16.

Shotwell, Alexis. 2011. *Knowing Otherwise: Race, Gender, and Implicit Understanding*. Pennsylvania State University Press.

———. 2017. "Forms of Knowing and Epistemic Resources." In *The Routledge Handbook of Epistemic Injustice*, edited by Ian James Kidd, José Medina, and Gaile Pohlhaus, 79–88. Routledge.

Smith, Carly Parnitzke, and Jennifer J. Freyd. 2013. "Dangerous Safe Havens: Institutional Betrayal Exacerbates Sexual Trauma." *Journal of Traumatic Stress* 26 (1): 119–124.

———. 2014. "Institutional Betrayal." *American Psychologist* 69 (6): 575–587. https://doi.org/10.1037/a0037564.

Smith, Roberta. 2014. "In a Mattress, a Lever for Art and Political Protest." *New York Times*, September 21.

Snowdon, Paul. 2004. "The Presidential Address: Knowing How and Knowing That: A Distinction Reconsidered." *Proceedings of the Aristotelian Society* 104 (no. 1): 1–29.

Solnit, Rebecca. 2017. *The Mother of All Questions.* Haymarket Books.

South African Truth and Reconciliation Commission. 1998. *Truth and Reconciliation Commission of South Africa Report.* Juta.

Stanley, Jason. 2011. *Know How.* Oxford University Press.

Stark, Samantha. 2018. "'I Kept Thinking of Antioch': Long Before #MeToo, a Times Video Journalist Remembered a Form She Signed in 2004." *New York Times*, April 8. https://www.nytimes.com/2018/04/08/insider/antioch-sexual-consent-form-metoo-video.html.

Stone, Jaclyn. 2020. "Receive, Respond, Report: Faculty Experiences with Students' Disclosures of Sexual Assault." PhD diss., University of Maryland, Baltimore County.

Strauss Swanson, Charlotte, and Dawn M. Szymanski. 2021. "Anti-Sexual Assault Activism and Positive Psychological Functioning Among Survivors." *Sex Roles* 85:25–38.

Stroud, Sarah. 2006. "Epistemic Partiality in Friendship." *Ethics* 116:498–524.

Sue, Derald Wing, Mikal N. Rasheed, and Janice Matthews Rasheed. 2015. *Multicultural Social Work Practice: A Competency-Based Approach to Diversity and Social Justice.* John Wiley.

Tatum, Beverly Daniel. 2007. *Can We Talk About Race? And Other Conversations in an Era of School Resegregation.* Beacon.

———. 2017. "'Why Are All the Black Kids Still Sitting Together in the Cafeteria?' And Other Conversations About Race in the Twenty-First Century." *Liberal Education* 103:46–56.

Tolman, Deborah L. 2012. "Female Adolescents, Sexual Empowerment and Desire: A Missing Discourse of Gender Inequity." *Sex Roles* 66 (11–12): 746–757. https://doi.org/10.1007/s11199-012-0122-x.

Tuerkheimer, Deborah. 2017. "Incredible Women: Sexual Violence and the Credibility Discount." *University of Pennsylvania Law Review* 166:1. https://doi.org/10.2139/ssrn.2919865.

Ullman, Sarah E., Erin O'Callaghan, Veronica Shepp, and Casey Harris. 2020. "Reasons for and Experiences of Sexual Assault Nondisclosure in a Diverse Community Sample." *Journal of Family Violence* 35 (8): 839–851. https://doi.org/10.1007/s10896-020-00141-9.

U.S. Department of Education, Office for Civil Rights. 2011a. "'Dear Colleague' Letter Guidance, Supplementing the OCR's Revised Sexual Harassment Guidance (2001)." http://www2.ed.gov/about/offices/list/ocr/letters/colleague201104.html.

———. 2011b. "Dear Colleague Letter: Sexual Violence: Background, Summary, and Fast Facts: (550302011–001)." https://doi.org/10.1037/e550302011-001.

———. 2021. "Summary of Major Provisions of the Department of Education's Title IX Final Rule." https://www.ed.gov/sites/ed/files/about/offices/list/ocr/docs/titleix-summary.pdf.

Vail, Katie. 2019. "The Failings of Title IX for Survivors of Sexual Violence: Utilizing Restorative Justice on College Campuses." *Washington Law Review* 94 (4).

van der Kolk, Bessel. 2014. *The Body Keeps Score: Brian, Mind, and Body in the Healing of Trauma*. Viking.

Vangelisti, Anita L. 1994. "Family Secrets: Forms, Functions and Correlates." *Journal of Social and Personal Relationships* 11 (1): 113–135. https://doi.org/10.1177/0265407594111007.

Vangelisti, Anita L., John Caughlin, and Lindsay Timmerman. 2001. "Criteria for Revealing Family Secrets." *Communication Monographs* 68 (1): 1–27.

Wade, Lisa. 2017. *American Hookup: The New Culture of Sex on Campus*. Norton.

Walker, Maureen. 2019. *When Getting Along Is Not Enough: Reconstructing Race in Our Lives and Relationships*. Teachers College Press.

Walker, Melanie. 2019. "Why Epistemic Justice Matters in and for Education." *Asia Pacific Education Review* 20:161–170.

Walsh, Wendy A., Victoria L. Banyard, Mary M. Moynihan, Sally Ward, and Ellen S. Cohn. 2010. "Disclosure and Service Use on a College Campus After an Unwanted Sexual Experience." *Journal of Trauma & Dissociation* 11 (2): 134–151. https://doi.org/10.1080/15299730903502912.

Waltzer, Tal, Riley L. Cox, Carina F. Moser, and Gail D. Heyman. 2024. "Don't Be a Rat: An Investigation of the Taboo Against Reporting Other Students for Cheating." *Journal of Experimental Child Psychology* 242:105894. https://doi.org/10.1016/j.jecp.2024.105894.

Wanderer, Jeremy. 2017. "Varieties of Testimonial Injustice." In *The Routledge Handbook of Epistemic Injustice*, edited by Ian James Kidd, José Medina, and Gaile Pohlhaus, 27–40. Routledge.

White House Task Force to Protect Students from Sexual Assault. 2014. *Not Alone*. https://obamawhitehouse.archives.gov/sites/default/files/docs/report_0.pdf

Williamsen, Kaaren M. and Erik S. Wessel, eds. 2023. *Applying Restorative Justice to Campus Sexual Misconduct: A Guide to Emerging Practices*. Routledge.

Yarinsky, Anna. 2018. "Anita Hill Speaks at Vanderbilt on the 'Rationing of Justice' Seen in Sexual Assault Cases and How We Can All Help Create Positive Change." *Vanderbilt Hustler,* October 29. https://vanderbilthustler.com/2018/10/29/anita-hill-speaks-at-vanderbilt-on-the-rationing-of-justice-seen-in-sexual-assault-cases-and-how-we-all-can-help-create-positive-change/.

Yin, Robert K. 2018. *Case Study Research and Applications: Design and Methods*. 6th ed. Sage.

Zerubavel, Eviatar. 2006. *The Elephant in the Room: Silence and Denial in Everyday Life*. Oxford University Press.

Index

About the Authors

JANET HINSON SHOPE is a professor of sociology at Goucher College in Baltimore, MD. Her research focuses on intimate partner violence, paid and unpaid work, and gender transitions to democracy. Her recent book, *Paid to Party*, examines the relationship between time and emotion for women working at home.

RICHARD (RICK) PRINGLE is an emeritus professor of psychology at Goucher College in Baltimore, MD whose primary interests are research methods, relational/transformative knowing, and social justice. In and outside his classes he used discursive circles, theater, memoir, journaling, and collaborative endeavors to explore lived experience and to challenge participants, including himself, to live into the moral implications of their expanding awareness.